The Hands of Day

Las manos del día

PABLO NERUDA
The Hands of Day

TRANSLATED BY WILLIAM O'DALY

COPPER CANYON PRESS

PORT TOWNSEND, WASHINGTON

Printed in the United States of America

Cover art: © iStockphoto.com / Duncan Walker

Copper Canyon Press is in residence at Fort Worden State
Park in Port Townsend, Washington, under the auspices of
Centrum. Centrum is a gathering place for artists and
creative thinkers from around the world, students of all ages
and backgrounds, and audiences seeking extraordinary
cultural enrichment.

LIBRARY OF CONGRESS CATALOGING-IN-PUBLICATION DATA
Neruda, Pablo, 1904–1973.
[Manos del día. English]
The hands of day / Pablo Neruda ; translated by
William O'Daly.
p. cm.
ISBN 978-1-55659-272-0 (pbk. : alk. paper)
I. O'Daly, William. II. Title.

PQ8097.N4M313 2008
861'.62—dc22

2008002014

COPPER CANYON PRESS
Post Office Box 271
Port Townsend, Washington 98368
www.coppercanyonpress.org

CONTENTS

Translator's Acknowledgments and a Note on the Original Edition

The Hands of Day is my seventh translation of Pablo Neruda's late and posthumous work, and I remain astonished and humbled by the spirit of collaboration among those who contribute to building a home for the original poems in the translations. For the quality of his commitment, his sensibility and precision, I am grateful to Reed Aubin for editorial contributions that brought the translation closer to the original and honored both. Professor Jaime Concha, of the University of California at San Diego, in his deeply informed responses to questions that can have no answers, shared with me his thoughts on some of the more layered passages. I thank Sam Hamill for encouraging the translation of this book never before published in English. To the staff at Copper Canyon Press, I extend my gratitude for their continued interest in this series of Neruda's late and posthumous works and for their expertise. For their generous support, which made possible this translation of *Las manos del día*, I am grateful to the National Endowment for the Arts.

My friend Terry Rivasplata brought me a bronze plaque given to him by his brother, Charles, who had discovered it in Chile. The plaque just so happens to contain the last six lines of the original Poem IX, "Destinies," speaking of the poet's friends and enemies:

"they partook of something and my life served them." Welcoming that message in a bottle from the motherland of Neruda, I offer a deep bow.

I thank my ten-year old daughter, Kyra Gray O'Daly, for transcribing the "Introduction," bundled up against autumn evenings' chill with her small lamp, and for her patient understanding. To my wife, Kristine, who impelled me to return to Neruda after many years away, whose belief and counsel are the bread of each day, my love and gratitude.

The original poems are taken from the Debolsillo edition, 2004, Buenos Aires, Argentina. That edition, with an introduction by Manuel Vázquez Montalbán, edited and with notes by Hernán Loyola, follows the text of the fourth Losada edition of Neruda's *Obras completas*, 1973, which contains revisions and corrections made by Neruda to the text of the first edition of *Las manos del día*, originally published in 1968.

Several of these translations were first published in *CutBank 65*.

Introduction

Pablo Neruda has long been celebrated as a poet of love and of the sea, of the people, of the rain, the stones and the birds, always keeping his formidable center through his transmigrations from one book to the next. With the publication of *Las manos del día* (*The Hands of Day*) in 1968, Neruda brought to full flower a recurrent theme that arises from the experiences and ideas that moved him to dedicate himself, as his friend and biographer Volodia Teitelboim describes, "to a life where places have been made for all to rightfully claim." Here Neruda grows ever stronger as a poet of the hand, the hand that joins the hammer and the nail, the minerals and the grinder, the threads of the fresh shirt and the bread of the street. Like the curved bridge or the snowy cordillera running between countries or the "wandering unity of life" honoring the water before it empties into the sea, don Pablo's hands integrate experience, intellect, intuition, and feeling into a poetry that unites peoples of different languages and cultures by giving voice to his longing and to theirs, to what we struggle against or become, what we must embrace or eventually betray.

Neruda begins with a sustained lament that he never made a broom, that his hands never gathered "the thread / of the broom" or laid "the tender stalks out to dry" or united them "in a golden bundle." Nor did he make a chair, so when the people of the world sit down at a wooden table or in the theater, not a single one will use a chair made by his shadow hands. As a poet, although the hands of the sea shaped him, teaching his fingers "the freedom of water," he did not make the sea. And yet every object he touches—whether it be the crystal glass filled with red wine or the ship's figurehead in his study, the sheet of paper or his desk chair—was made by someone else's hands. Much has been said about the poet's feelings of guilt at not having contributed material comforts to the many who sustained him, or to their sustenance or their passion.

> within that nobody I am
> one worthless servant,
> like a mollusk cracked
> by the teeth of the sea.

These sometimes excessive feelings of guilt arise from Neruda's desire to do everything, to contribute to and participate in the motion of "pine needles sewing 'another day to the night.'" They represent a cluster of engagements and beliefs that he converts, according to Manuel Vázquez Montalbán, into a "splendid poetry of banishment." Even as he writes poems by hand, on white paper and with green ink, crossing the provinces on the train or sitting in his backyard, orchestrated moments of overstatement often are followed by a delicate touch, albeit one capable of sustaining the cumulative power of hands joined in some clarity of motion, generating a "rose of energy." The life that the poet imagines for himself is a near opposite of the one he leads, a life he sometimes characterizes as akin to consciousness in death, in order to compose his gift. His disappointment in himself and feelings of shame, his accomplishments as he grows used "to dying more than one death," create the atmospheric conditions by which the book's supporting themes manifest as blood, bread, snow, pursuit and absence, seeking, navigating, and going astray. These themes develop as alternating currents, cycling through and eventually merging in a "circuit of hands," in the book's sixty-eight intimately related poems.

Above all else in *The Hands of Day*, the beloved Chilean poet celebrates the transformative powers of *others'* hands, of those who build with wood or metal or who harvest the grain or the fish, of those who make the wine, and of the powerful hands he entreats to help him change the profile of the planets, to shape the triangular stars the traveler needs. He also meditates on the role of the writer, chastises those who attacked him mercilessly for personal gain rather than focusing their energies on creating work and lives of greater integrity, and he implicates himself among those artists who carry like a "small beast" on their shoulders the capacity for self-delusion. As the singer of others' lives, a poet often lost in the sound of his own voice as he walks amid the fragrance of "the sacred forest," he nevertheless is rooted in the earth like the purest autumn or the humid springtime—melancholic, playful, acerbic at times and always fresh, touching the bells and the hope, the dreams and the suffering, and, ultimately, his happiness in solidarity.

One can sense in these poems a new incarnation of Neruda's lifelong desire to break out of his "limited world" (to use his term), in order to branch out like the forests and the rivers of his birth. In his memoirs, Neruda writes that he does not remember exactly how or when he encountered the poetry of Walt Whitman, but that it was a life-altering experience. That seminal poet of the same hemisphere who helped him along this road was poetic and political seed scattered decades before the composition of this late book and took root as Neruda reoriented and expanded his engagement with poetry and his role as a poet. His poetic kinship with Whitman, as well as his close friendships with Federico García Lorca, Rafael Alberti, Miguel

Hernández, and other Spanish poets in the years before the disastrous Spanish Civil War, certainly helped to transform his earlier isolating experiences as a young Chilean consul in Burma, Ceylon, all those alien places that had given rise to "the same absent silk and the same cold fiber" of *Residence on Earth* (*Residencia en la tierra*). In his "Ode to Walt Whitman," Neruda refers to his "first cousin": "I touched a hand and it was / the hand of Walt Whitman." In *The Hands of Day,* Neruda follows Whitman's lead by affirming that, despite his many failings, he has worked with the material he was given, with what he is, remaining true to himself and his commitments as a poet. We find an expression of this in Poem IX, "Destinies," which may be considered a brief *ars poetica,* one of two found in the book. The poet speaks of the customhouse at the passage between life and death, where one day someone will ask how many things he "cultivated, carved, composed . . . between hungry and mortal hands." He answers, "this is what I made, it is this which we made."

> *Because I felt that in some way*
> *I shared what they made,*
> *my brothers or my enemies:*
> *and they, of so much nothingness that I pulled*
> *out of nothing, out of my nothingness,*
> *they partook of something and my life served them.*

In this merging of needs and energies, he begins to lay the groundwork for the "constructive synthesis," as Sr. Montalbán calls it in his introduction to the original poems, one that must avoid transfiguring the poet's persona as the hero. After all, he who is a child of the moon is not a hero for wanting to be a part of the light, regardless of the form his happiness takes, nor is he a hero for finally coming to accept what he is. Few readers of Neruda are surprised when they encounter, again in his memoirs, "We poets have a right to be happy, as long as we are close to the people of our country and in the thick of the fight for their happiness." "You cannot be happy," he told a journalist from *El Mercurio* in 1969, "if you don't fight for the happiness of others. You can never lose the sense of guilt at having something if others don't have it also. Man cannot be a happy island." On the contrary, as he says in the poem "We Drown": "we have a duty to bear with the others / and to fall down, to ford the river, in others' blood." It is largely in the fulfillment of this duty to build with others what benefits all that the poet discovers what makes him happy.

After writing his only play, *Splendor and Death of Joaquin Murieta* (1967), Neruda participated firsthand in the camaraderie of those preparing for the stage. *The Hands of Day,* arriving in the afterglow of that creative collaboration, achieves that connection in the confessional tones of a gently sonorous, self-aware romanticism, which at times resides in the southern hemisphere of the real to capture with terrestrial precision what cannot be seen or named. The surreal touch is more a natural extension of the poet's worldview—the result of conscious interaction with the elements and their relationships to one another and the whole—than it is borne by any stylistic choice. It is what Neruda describes as "guided spontaneity," arising from a sensibility much closer to his beautiful friend Paul Éluard's than to Apollinaire's.

> As with worn-out knives
> the handle and the blade grow thin,
> they change to the touch,
> I have seen this day return
> from a long journey through night
> turned into a blue knife,
> tool of the moon.

In the poem "The Weeping," Neruda casts his net over human vulnerabilities and shortcomings, those uniting us in this world that our hands create for one another. We live beside ourselves, we get in our own way, we fail to appreciate what makes us genuinely happy. We beseech the world to fulfill our cravings at the expense of knowing ourselves. On the other hand, when the reader arrives at "I Know Nothing," the link between the manual laborer and the poet who composes work by hand firmly establishes that "everything / begins with words."

> new words that sit alone
> at the table, not having been invited,
> hateful words that we swallow
> and that get into our cupboards,
> our beds, our loves,
> until they exist: until the beginning
> begins again in the verb.

From his role as a poet who simply wants to make things comes his contempt for "Pavín Cerdo" of the poem "Early" and his antipathy toward "El Mapús, el Mapís . . ." of the poem "Bad Writers." The former is identified by Hernán Loyola, in his notes on the original poems, as an allusion to the writer and journalist Hernán Lavín Cerda, of *Punto Final* magazine (an arm of Movimiento de Izquierda Revolucionaria de Chile), "who could not hide his antipathy toward Neruda on account of his being a figure and symbol of the Chilean Communist Party and who never missed an occasion to criticize him from an ultra left-wing position." The latter is an allusion, according to Sr. Loyola, to Mahfúd Massís, son-in-law of the poet Pablo de Rokha and his loyal henchman in their fierce hatred of Neruda. Not long after Neruda arrived in Santiago from his home in the South, he and other young poets fell under the wing of the egotistical, dictatorial, and increasingly eccentric de Rokha, who never forgave him for leaving the fold or for eclipsing his reputation as a leading poet of Chile.

On a more loving note, Poem XLIII, "J.S.," is a tribute to the enigmatic and shy Jorge Sanhueza, who from 1954 to 1967, when he quietly died in a hospital room at age forty-three, was the curator of Neruda's archives at the Central Library of the University of Chile. Described by Sr. Teitelboim as an "unobtrusive presence" in Neruda's life, "who comes and goes pronouncing cryptic phrases and then almost dissolves into the sensation of absence," Sanhueza acted as a secretary to Neruda and left a biography of him unfinished. While certainly there are many writers the likes of Hernán Lavín Cerda and Mahfúd Massís—capitalists of the soul who possess little more than daggers—there are also the literary workers such as Jorge Sanhueza, and even the poet himself, which is all the more reason to celebrate competency, hard work, and the simple gifts of an iron spatula or a broom.

Hence, what those who seek the light, true companionship, and the solidarity of positive hands must do, as they bear the past in their intentions and work to create a better future for all, is recognize the value of the "shard of a pot or of a flag / or simply a notion of light, / algae of the aquarium of night, / a fiber that did not waste away, / pure doggedness, air of gold." There is little room between dying and being born again, and we must commit ourselves to living on the frontier of our lives, moving within the cyclic light, round as a ring. The days come and go, the bad and the good, in the marriage of elements and consciousness that define our humanity and are really all we have.

> Thin layer of volcano, petal of hatred,
> carnivorous throat,
> such is a day, and the next one

is tenderly,
yes, resolutely, a wedding song.

Embracing his nature and striving for unity within and without, Neruda accepts his investiture as a poet and a man. He finds, among his contributions, his fellow human beings and his teachers, those elements that compose the unity of the grape and darkness in the company of light.

This is my glass, do you see
the blood shine
beyond the edge of the crystal?
This is my glass, I drink
to the unity
of the wine,
to the harvested light,
to my destiny and other destinies,
to what I had and what I did not have,
and to the blood-colored sword that sings
with the transparent glass.

In the penultimate poem, "The Gift," the reader arrives at the book's second *ars poetica,* an integration of Neruda's social and political values with the man he is, bearing his insecurities and his courage in confronting the seductions and corruptions of those who would undermine the unity he has worked so hard to create. He has not retreated, and by refusing to do so he shares with those he so admires his hope for the present day and for the future.

I want all the hands of men
to knead mountains
of bread and to gather
all the fish from the sea,
all the olives

from the olive tree,
all the love not yet wakened
and to leave a gift
in each of the hands
of the day.

WILLIAM O'DALY
AUTUMN 2007

The Hands of Day

Las manos del día

I

El culpable

Me declaro culpable de no haber
hecho, con estas manos que me dieron,
una escoba.

Por qué no hice una escoba?

Por qué me dieron manos?

Para qué me sirvieron
si sólo vi el rumor del cereal,
si sólo tuve oídos para el viento
y no recogí el hilo
de la escoba,
verde aún en la tierra,
y no puse a secar los tallos tiernos
y no los pude unir
en un haz áureo
y no junté una caña de madera
a la falda amarilla
hasta dar una escoba a los caminos?

Así fue:
no sé cómo
se me pasó la vida
sin aprender, sin ver,
sin recoger y unir
los elementos.

I
THE GUILTY ONE

I declare myself guilty of never having
fashioned, with these hands I was given,
a broom.

Why did I not make a broom?

Why was I given hands at all?

What purpose did they serve
if I saw only the rumor of the grain,
if I had ears only for the wind
and did not gather the thread
of the broom,
still green on the earth,
and did not lay the tender stalks out to dry
and was not able to unite them
in a golden bundle
or attach a wooden cane
to the yellow skirt
so I had a broom to sweep the paths.

So it was:
I do not know how
I lived my life
without learning, without seeing,
without gathering and uniting
those elements.

En esta hora no niego
que tuve tiempo,
tiempo,
pero no tuve manos,
y así, cómo podía
aspirar con razón a la grandeza
si nunca fui capaz
de hacer
una escoba,
una sola,
una?

At this hour I cannot deny
I had the time,
time,
but not the hands,
and so, how could I aspire
with my mind to greatness
and not be capable
of making
a broom,
not one,
one?

II
El vacío

Y cómo se hace el mar?
Yo no hice el mar:
lo encontré en sus salvajes
oficinas,
lo hallé dispuesto a todo,
crepitante,
pacífico,
atlántico de plomo,
mediterráneo
teñido de anilina,
todo era blanco y hondo,
hirviente y permanente,
tenía olas, ovarios,
naves muertas,
latía
su organismo.

Lo medí entre las rocas
de la tierra asombrada
y dije, no lo hice,
no lo hice yo, ni nadie:
en ese nadie soy
un sirviente inservible,
como un molusco roto
por los dientes del mar.

No hice la sal dispersa
ni el viento coronado
por la racha que rompe la blancura
no, no hice

II
EMPTINESS

And how is a sea made?
I did not make the sea:
I discovered it in its wild
offices,
I found it ready for anything,
crackling,
pacific,
atlantic of lead,
mediterranean
dyed with aniline:
everything was white and deep,
seething and forever,
it had waves, ovaries,
dead ships:
its body
was pulsing.

I measured it between the rocks
of the astonished earth
and said, I did not make it,
no, I did not make it, nobody did:
within that nobody I am
one worthless servant,
like a mollusk cracked
by the teeth of the sea.

I did not make the scattered salt
nor the wind crowned
by the gust that shatters the whiteness,
no, I did not make

la luz del agua ni el beso que estremece
la nave con sus labios de batalla,
ni las demoliciones de la arena,
ni el movimiento que envolvió en silencio
a la ballena y sus procreaciones.

Yo fui alejado
de estos infinitos:
ni un solo dedo de mis semejantes
tembló en el agua urgiendo la existencia
y vine a ser testigo
de la más tempestuosa soledad
sin más que ojos vacíos
que se llenaron de olas
y que se cerrarán
en el vacío.

the water's light nor the kiss that shakes
the ship with embattled lips,
nor the explosions of sand,
nor the movement that wrapped in silence
the whale and its children.

I was removed
from those infinities,
not a single finger of my fellow man
trembled in the water that hastens existence,
and I came to be a witness
to the most turbulent solitude
with nothing more than empty eyes
that filled with waves
and will close
on emptiness.

III

A SENTARSE

Todo el mundo sentado
a la mesa,
en el trono,
en la asamblea,
en el vagón del tren,
en la capilla,
en el océano,
en el avión, en la escuela, en el estadio
todo el mundo sentado o sentándose,
pero no habrá recuerdos
de una silla
que hayan hecho mis manos.

Qué pasó? Por qué, si mi destino
me llevó a estar sentado, entre otras cosas,
por qué no me dejaron
implantar cuatro patas
de un árbol extinguido
al asiento, al respaldo,
a la persona próxima
que allí debió aguardar el nacimiento
o la muerte de alguna que él amaba?
La silla que no pude, que no hice,
transformando en estilo
la naturalidad de la madera
y en aparato claro
el rito de los árboles sombríos.

La sierra circular
como un planeta

III
SITTING DOWN

The whole world sitting
at the table,
on the throne,
at the assembly,
in the train car,
in the chapel,
on the ocean,
in the plane, in the school, in the stadium
the whole world being seated or seating themselves:
but they will have no memory
of any chair
made by my hands.

What happened? Why, if my destiny
was, among other things, to sit down,
why was I not allowed
to plant four legs
of an extinguished tree
into the seat, into the back,
for the very next person
who had to await the birth
or the death of someone he loved?
I failed the chairs, never built one,
transforming in its style
the naturalness of the wood
and in its illustrious form
the rite of the dark trees.

The circular saw
like a planet

descendió de la noche
hasta la tierra
y rodó por los montes
de mi patria,
pasó sin ver por mi puerta larvaria,
se perdió en su sonido
y así fue como anduve
en el aroma
de la selva sagrada
sin agredir con hacha la arboleda,
sin tomar en mis manos
la decisión y la sabiduría
de cortar el ramaje
y extraer
una silla
de la inmovilidad
y repetirla
hasta que esté sentado todo el mundo.

descended the night
until it reached the earth.
It rolled through the mountains
of my country,
it passed, without seeing, through my door of larvae,
it became lost in its own sound,
and that was how I walked
in the fragrance
of the sacred forest
without taking a hatchet to the thicket of small trees,
without taking in my hands
the decision and the wisdom
of cutting off the branches
and bringing forth
from stillness
a chair
and repeating it
until the whole world is sitting down.

IV
LAS MANOS NEGATIVAS

Cuándo me vio ninguno
cortado tallos, aventando el trigo?
Quién soy, si no hice nada?
Cualquiera, hijo de Juan,
tocó el terreno
y dejó caer algo
que entró como la llave
entra en la cerradura
y la tierra se abrió de par en par.

Yo no, no tuve tiempo,
ni enseñanza:
guardé las manos limpias
del cadáver urbano,
me despreció la grasa de las ruedas,
el barro inseparable de las costumbres claras
se fue a habitar sin mí las provincias silvestres:
la agricultura nunca se ocupó de mis libros
y sin tener qué hacer, perdido en las bodegas,
reconcentré mis pobres preocupaciones
hasta que no viví sino en las despedidas.

Adiós dije al aceite, sin conocer la oliva,
y al tonel, un milagro de la naturaleza,
dije también adiós porque no comprendía
cómo se hicieron tantas cosas sobre la tierra
sin el consentimiento de mis manos inútiles.

IV
NEGATIVE HANDS

When did anyone ever see me
cutting branches, winnowing the wheat?
Who am I, if I created nothing?
Anyone, any son of a Juan
could touch the land
and let fall something
that entered as a key
enters the lock,
and the earth would open wide.

Not me, I did not have the time
or the skill:
I kept my hands clean
as those of a city cadaver,
even axle grease despised me,
the mud, inseparable from rustic customs,
left without me to inhabit the wild provinces:
plowing the soil never had a place in my books
and not having made that place, lost among wine cellars,
I concealed my poor obsessions
till I only really lived in farewells.

Goodbye, I called to the oil, without knowing the olive,
and to the barrel, that miracle of nature,
I said goodbye, for I could not comprehend
how so many things were made on earth
without the consent of my useless hands.

V

EL OLVIDO

Manos que sólo ropas y cuerpos
trabajaron,
camisas y caderas
y libros, libros, libros
hasta que sólo fueron
manos de sombra, redes
sin peces, en el aire:
sólo certificaron
el heroísmo de las otras manos,
y la procreadora construcción
que dedos muertos levantaron
y continúan dedos vivos.

No hay *antes* en mis manos:
olvidé los labriegos
que en el transcurso
de mi sangre
araron:
no mandaron en mí las recias razas
de herreros
que mano a mano elaboraron
anclas, martillos, clavos,
cucharas y tenazas,
tornillos, rieles, lanzas,
locomotoras, proas,
para que ferroviarios fogoneros
con lentitud de manos sucias
de grasa y de carbón, fueran de pronto
dioses del movimiento

V
Forgetting

Hands that worked with only
clothes and bodies,
shirts and hips
and books, books, books
until they were merely
shadow hands, nets
without fish, in the air:
alone they attested to
the heroism of other hands
and the generative edifices
that dead fingers raised
and living fingers extend.

There is no *before* with my hands:
I forgot the peasants
who in the coursing
of my blood
plowed:
it was not blacksmiths
who ruled within me, sturdy people
who hand after hand fashioned
anchors, hammers, nails,
spoons and tongs,
screws, rails, lances,
locomotives, prows,
so that railroad stokers
with the slowness of hands filthy
with grease and coal, were suddenly
gods of motion

en los trenes que cruzan por mi infancia
bajo las manos verdes de la lluvia.

of trains that passed through my childhood
beneath the green hands of the rain.

VI
UNA CASA

Alguien toca una piedra y luego estalla
la piedra y los pedazos
se amalgaman de nuevo:
es la tarea
de los jóvenes dioses expulsados
del jardín solitario.
Es la tarea de
romper, restablecer,
quebrar, pegar, vencer
hasta que aquella roca
obedeció a las manos de Aguilera,
a los ojos de Antonio y Recaredo,
a la cabeza de don Alejandro.

Así se hacen las casas en la costa.

Y luego entran y salen las pisadas.

VI
A House

Someone touches a stone and the stone
explodes and the pieces
come back together again:
it is the work
of young gods expelled
from the solitary garden.
It is the work of
breaking, restoring again,
smashing, gluing together, conquering
until that rock
yielded to the hands of Aguilera,
the eyes of Antonio and Recaredo,
the head of don Alejandro.

That is how the houses on the coast are made.

And later the footsteps come and go.

VII
El frío

Mirad los pedernales de Aconcagua:
brillan millones de ojos en la nieve,
millones de miradas.

Está dormido sin embargo
el universo duro:
falta el rápido rayo,
el movimiento.

Entonces unas manos
abren el pecho amargo
de la altura
y dos piedras se besan,
se enlazan
hasta que una pequeña chispa ciega
todavía
sale sin rumbo y vuela
y otra cae y se une
al movimiento
del humo, allá en las cumbres
de Aconcagua.

Frío, padre del fuego!

VII

The Cold

Look upon the silica of Aconcagua:
millions of eyes shine in the snow,
millions of expressions.

Even so, the hard universe
is sleeping:
the rapid flash is absent,
the movement.

Then some hands
open the bitter breast
of the heights
and two stones kiss,
they connect
until a small blind spark
rises still
without its bearings and flies
then falls and joins
the drift
of the smoke, there among the peaks
of Aconcagua.

Cold, father of the fire!

VIII

El campanero

Aun aquel que volvió
del monte, de la arena,
del mar, del mineral, del agua
con las manos vacías,
aun el domador
que volvió del caballo
en un cajón, quebrado
y fallecido,
o la mujer de siete manos
que en el telar
perdió de pronto el hilo
y regresó al ovario
a no ser más que harapo,
o aun el campañero
que al mover
en la cuerda
el firmamento
cayó de las iglesias
hacia la oscuridad
y el cementerio:
aun todos ellos
se fueron
con las manos gastadas
no por la suavidad sino por algo:
el tiempo corrosivo,
la substancia
enemiga
del carbón, de la ola,

VIII

THE BELL RINGER

Even the one who returned
from the mountain, from the sand,
from the sea, from the mineral, from the water
with empty hands,
even the trainer
who returned from the horse
in his coffin, broken
and deceased,
or the woman of seven hands
who on her loom
soon lost the thread
and returned to the ovary,
to nothing more than a tatter,
or even the bell ringer
who pulled
on the rope
so the firmament
fell from the churches
toward the darkness
and the cemetery:
even they all
departed
with hands exhausted,
not by smoothness but by something else:
corrosive time,
the inimical
essence
of the coal, of the wave,

del algodón, del viento,
porque sólo el dolor enseñó a ser:
porque hacer fue el destino de las manos
y en cada cicatriz cabe la vida.

of the cotton, of the wind,
because sadness alone taught us to be:
because to build was the destiny of hands
and every scar holds life within it.

IX
DESTINOS

De tu destino dame una bandera,
un terrón, una espátula de fierro,
algo que vuele o pase, la cintura
de una vasija, el sol de una cebolla:
te lo pido por cuanto no hice nada.
Y antes de despedirme, quiero estar
preparado y llegar con tus trabajos
como si fueran míos, a la muerte.
Allí en la aduana me preguntarán
cuántas cosas labré, corté, compuse,
remendé, completé, dejé moviendo
entre manos hambrientas y mortales
y yo responderé:
esto es lo que hice, es esto lo que hicimos.

Porque sentí que de alguna manera
compartí lo que hacían
o mis hermanos o mis enemigos:
y ellos, de tanta nada que saqué
de la nada, de la nada mía,
tomaron algo y les sirvió mi vida.

IX

DESTINIES

From your destiny give me a flag,
a lump of earth, a spatula of iron,
something that flies or passes by, the waist
of a clay pot, the sun of an onion:
I ask this of you, for how much of nothing I made.
But before you send me on my way, I want to be
prepared and with the things you made
arrive at death, as if they were mine.
There in the customhouse they will ask me
how many things I cultivated, carved, composed,
repaired, finished, left moving
between hungry and mortal hands,
and I will answer:
this is what I made, it is this which we made.

Because I felt that in some way
I shared what they made,
my brothers or my enemies:
and they, of so much nothingness that I pulled
out of nothing, out of my nothingness,
they partook of something and my life served them.

X

El viajero

Cuando muy joven me extravié en el mundo,
cruzando, derrotado, los caminos.
Era iracunda y áspera la noche,
la noche con espinas de la selva.

Descubrí un desmedido pie de piedra:
un pie de piedra blanca como un monte
quebrado en el tobillo, y la blancura
del pie, de aquellos dedos enterrados,
de aquella planta hundida entre raíces,
no fue sólo misterio para mí.

Me sentí desdeñado,
mucho más enterrado y cercenado
que el gran vestigio blanco
del dios ausente escondido en la selva.

X
The Traveler

When I was very young I went astray in the world,
crossing, nearly ruined, the roads.
The night was angry and harsh,
the night of jungle thorns.

I discovered a misshapen foot of stone:
a stone foot white as a mountain
broken at the ankle, and the whiteness
of the foot, of those buried toes,
of that plant sunk among roots,
was, for me, not just a mystery.

I was filled with disdain,
more buried and cut off
than the great white remains
of the absent god hidden in the forest.

XI

AUSENTES

No hay nadie. Unos golpearon todo el día
la misma rueda hasta que ahora rueda,
otros cubrieron de lástex el mundo
hasta dejarlo verde,
anaranjado,
violeta
y amarillo.

Éstos vuelven del mar y ya se fueron.

Aquí estuvieron sin parar las manos
sacudiendo en el aire la blancura
las lavanderas, pero ya se fueron.

Y los que manejaron el alambre
o las locomotoras,
hasta los sacerdotes
del crepúsculo
todos tomaron el mismo navío,
todos se fueron entre tantas olas
de la noche
o con el polvo amargo del desierto
o con la combustión de las estrellas
o con el agua que se va y no vuelve
o con el llanto que busca a los muertos,
todos hicieron algo, y es de noche.

Yo navego perdido
entre la soledad que me dejaron.

———

XI
The Absent Ones

There is no one. All day several hammered
the same wheel until it was a wheel,
others covered the world with Lastex
until it was green,
orange,
violet,
and yellow.

These return from the sea and soon are gone.

Here were hands in ceaseless motion
the washerwomen shaking the whiteness
in the air, but soon they were gone.

And those that handled wire
or locomotives,
even the priests
of the last light
all boarded the same ship,
they all departed among so many waves
of the night
or with the bitter dust of the desert
or with the burning of the stars
or with the water that flows and never returns
or with the weeping that searches for the dead,
they all made something, and it is of the night.

Lost, I navigate
in the solitude they left me.

Y como no hice nada,
miro en la oscuridad hacia tantas ausencias
que paulatinamente me han convertido en sombra.

And because I made nothing,
I stare in the darkness toward so many absences
that have slowly turned me into shadow.

XII
Astro en el día

Oh sol lleno de uñas,
animal de oro, abeja,
perro pastor del mundo,
perdona
el extravío,
ya llegamos, volvimos,
todos juntos
ya estamos esperando
en el corral del día.

Si desobedecimos esa noche,
si nos fuimos al sueño de la luna
a resolver el luto y los planetas,
si nos reconcentramos
en nuestra propia piel
hambrienta
de amor y de comida,
aquí estamos
de nuevo
en el redil,
obedeciendo
a tus largas espátulas de luz,
a tus dedos que se meten en todo,
a tu concubinato de semillas.

Ya se pusieron todos a moverse,
a correr. Ciudadano,
el día es corto y ahí está el sol como un toro
pataleando en la arena:
corra a buscar su pala,

XII
STAR IN DAYLIGHT

O sun full of fingernails,
animal of gold, bumblebee,
sheepdog of the world,
forgive
our going astray,
we have arrived, we return,
we are already waiting
all together
in the corral of day.

Say we disobeyed that night,
say we left it to the sleep of the moon
to solve the mourning and the planets,
say we withdraw into ourselves,
into our own skin hungry
for love and a meal,
we again are
here
in the sheepfold,
obeying
your long spatulas of light,
your fingers that reach into everything,
your cohabitation of seeds.

Soon everyone set about moving,
hurrying. Citizen,
the day is short and there the sun is like a bull
kicking in the sand:
hurry in search of your shovel,

su palanca,
su artesa,
su termómetro,
su pito, su pincel o sus tijeras,
su esparadrapo,
su montacargas, su buró politico,
sus papas en el mercado:
corra, señora, corra
caballero,
por aquí, por acá, mueva las manos,
se nos acaba la luz.

El sol llenó de estacas la alegría,
la esperanza, el padecimiento
se fue de un lado a otro con sus rayos
delimitando, atribuyendo tierras,
y cada uno tiene que sudar,
antes de que se vaya
con su luz a otra parte
a comenzar y comenzar de nuevo
mientras los de este lado se quedaron
inmóviles, dormidos,
hasta mañana lunes.

your lever,
your kneading trough,
your thermometer,
your whistle, your paintbrush or your scissors,
your plaster,
your freight elevator, your political bureau,
your potatoes at the market:
hurry, Ma'am, hurry
Mister,
over here, this way, put your hands to good use,
we are running out of daylight.

The sun, with stakes, pierced joy,
hope, suffering,
it traveled from one side to the other with its rays
parceling out, attributing lands,
and everyone has to sweat
before it leaves
with its light for somewhere else
to begin and begin again,
while those on this side remained
motionless, sleeping
until Monday morning.

XIII

El hijo de la luna

Todo está aquí viviendo,
haciendo,
haciéndose
sin participación de mi paciencia
y cuando colocaron estos rieles,
hace cien años,
yo no toqué este frío:
no levantó mi corazón mojado
por las lluvias del cielo de Cautín
un solo movimiento
que ayudara
a extender los caminos
de la velocidad que iba naciendo.

Ni luego puse un dedo
en la carrera
del público especial que mis amigos
lanzaron hacia Aldebarán suntuoso.

Y de los organismos egoístas
que sólo oyeron, vieron
y siguieron
yo sufrí humillaciones que no cuento
para que nadie siga sollozando
con mis versos que ya no tienen llanto
sino energía que gasté en el viento,
en el polvo, en la piedra del camino.

Y porque anduve tanto sin quebrar
los minerales ni cortar madera

XIII

CHILD OF THE MOON

Everything is here, living,
creating,
creating itself,
without my patient participation
and when they laid these rails,
a hundred years ago,
I did not touch this cold:
my heart, wet from the rains of Cautín,
did not give rise
to a single beat
that helped
build out the roads
for the speed being born.

Nor did I lift a finger
in the race
for the public space that my friends
launched toward sumptuous Aldebarán.

And at the hands of those egotistical organisms
that only listened, observed
and followed,
I suffered humiliations I will not relate
so nobody goes on sobbing
with my verses which have run out of tears,
which contain only the energy I wasted on the wind,
in the dust, on the stones of the road.

And because I went so far without grinding
minerals or cutting wood

siento que no me pertenece el mundo:
que es de los que clavaron y cortaron
y levantaron estos edificios
porque si la argamasa, que nació
y duró sosteniendo los designios,
la hicieron otras manos,
sucias de barro y sangre,
yo no tengo derecho a proclamar
mi existencia: fui un hijo de la luna.

I feel that the world does not belong to me:
it belongs to those who pounded nails and cut
and raised these buildings,
because if the mortar, which was born
and lasted sustaining the intentions,
was made by others' hands
caked with mud and blood,
I did not have the right to declare
that I existed: I was a child of the moon.

XIV

LA MANO CENTRAL

Tocar la acción, vivir la transparencia
del cristal en el fuego,
circular en el bronce
hasta cantar por boca de campana,
olorosa alegría
de la tabla que gime
como un violín
en el aserradero,
polvo del pan
que viaja
desde una rumorosa
conversación de espigas
hasta la máquina
de los panaderos,
tocar la desventura
del carbón
en su muerta catarata
sometido al latido
de las excavaciones
hasta quebrarse, huir,
aliarse y revivir
en el acero
tomando la unidad
de la pureza, la paloma ovalada
del nuevo movimiento,
acción,
acción de sangre,
circulación del fuego,

XIV
THE CENTRAL HAND

To take action, to live the transparency
of the crystal in the fire,
to circulate in bronze
until singing through the bell's mouth,
fragrant joy
of the table that whines
like a violin
in the sawmill,
dust of the bread
that drifts
from a rustling
conversation of spikes of grain
to the machinery
of the bakers,
touching the hard luck
of the coal
in its dead cataract
submitting to the beating
of the excavations
until breaking, escaping,
becoming an ally and living again
in the steel
taking on the unity
of purity, of the oval dove
of new motion,
action,
action of blood,
circulation of the fire,

circuito de las manos,
rosa de la energía.

circuit of hands,
rose of energy.

XV
Ciclo

Se repite una vez, más hacia el fondo,
la húmeda primavera:
mete los dedos entre las raíces
toca el hombre escondido.

Yo dormía allá abajo,
yo dormía.

Abre sus labios verdes,
se levanta:
es hombre, o planta, o río,
es ávida cintura,
es boca de agua.

Llegó la hora,
existo,
soy de luz y de arena.

Quién viene a verme? Nadie!

Yo soy nadie.

Y por qué este aire azul?

Yo soy azul.

En la rama una rosa?

Yo la enciendo.

XV
CYCLE

It repeats itself once, the humid springtime
closer to the depths:
it sinks its fingers among the roots,
it touches the hidden man.

I was sleeping there below,
I was sleeping.

It opens its green lips,
it rises up:
it is man, or plant, or river,
it is eager waist,
it is mouth of water.

The hour has arrived,
I exist,
I am of light and of sand.

Who comes to see me? No one!

I am no one.

And why this blue air?

I am blue.

On the stem a rose?

I set it ablaze.

XVI
Adioses

Yo no encendí sino un papel amargo.

Yo no fui causa de aquel Buenos Días
que se dieron el trueno con la rosa.

Yo no hice el mundo, no hice los relojes,
no hice las olas ni tampoco espero
hallar en las espigas mi retrato.

Y de tanto perder donde no estuve
fui quedándome ausente
sin derrochar ninguna preferencia
sino un monte de sal desmoronado
por una copa de agua del invierno.

Se pregunta el viajero si sostuvo
el tiempo, andando contra la distancia,
y vuelve adonde comenzó a llorar,
vuelve a gastar su dosis de yo mismo,
vuelve a irse con todos sus adioses.

XVI

GOODBYES

I burned nothing but a bitter sheet of paper.

I was not the cause of that "Good morning"
exchanged between the thunderclap and the rose.

I did not make the world, did not make the clocks,
did not make the waves, nor do I expect
to find my portrait among the grain.

And from losing so much where I wasn't
I continued to stay away,
not squandering any predilection
but a mountain of salt washed away
by a glass of winter water.

The traveler wonders whether he kept
time, walking to counter the distance,
and he returns to where he began to cry,
he returns to swallow his dose of me myself I,
he returns, leaving with all his goodbyes.

XVII

CERCA DE LOS CUCHILLOS

Es ésta el alma suave que esperaba,
ésta es el alma de hoy, sin movimiento,
como si estuviera hecha de luna
sin aire, quieta en su bondad terrible.

Cuando caiga una piedra
como un puño
del cielo de la noche
en esta copa la recibiré:
en la luz rebosante
recibiré la oscuridad viajera,
la incertidumbre celeste.

No robaré sino este movimiento
de la hierba del cielo,
de la noche fértil:
sólo un golpe de fuego,
una caída.

Líbrame, tierra oscura, de mis llaves:
si pude abrir y refrenar
y volver a cerrar el cielo duro,
doy testimonio de que no fui nada,
de que no fui nadie,
de que no fui.

Solo esperé la estrella,
el dardo de la luna,
el rayo de piedra celeste,
esperé inmóvil en la sociedad

XVII

Close to the Knives

It is this, the smooth soul that was waiting,
this is the soul of today, unmoving,
as though it were made of moonlight
without air, still in its terrifying kindness.

Whenever a stone falls
like a fist
of the sky at night
into this glass I will welcome it:
within the overflowing light
I will welcome the traveling darkness,
the heavenly uncertainty.

I will steal only this movement
from the grass of the sky,
from the fertile night:
only a strike of fire,
a single fall.

Free me, dark earth, from my keys:
even were I able to open and rein in,
and return to close the hard sky,
I testify to being nothing,
to being no one,
to not being.

I waited only for the star,
the dart of the moon,
the ray of celestial stone,
I waited motionless in the society

de la hierba que crece en primavera,
de la leche en la ubre,
de la miel perezosa y peregrina:
esperé la esperanza,
y aquí estoy
convicto
de haber pactado con la tempestad,
de haber aceptado la ira,
de haber abierto el alma,
de haber oído entrar al asesino,
mientras yo conversaba con la noche.

Ahí viene otro, dijo ladrando el perro.

Y yo con mis ojos de frío,
con el luto plateado
que me dio el firmamento,
no vi el puñal ni el perro,
no escuché los ladridos.

Y aquí estoy cuando nacen las semillas
y se abren como labios:
todo es fresco y profundo.

Estoy muerto,
estoy asesinado:
estoy naciendo
con la primavera.

Aquí tengo una hoja,
una oreja, un susurro,
un pensamiento:
voy a vivir otra vez,

of grass that grows in spring,
of milk in the udder,
of lazy and migrating honey:
I waited for hope,
and here I am
convicted
of having made a pact with the tempest,
of having accepted the anger,
of having opened the soul,
of having heard the assassin enter,
even as I was conversing with the night.

Here comes another, said the barking dog.

And I with my eyes of cold,
with silver grief
the firmament gave me,
I did not see the dagger or the dog,
I did not listen to the barking.

And I am here when the seeds are born
and open like lips:
everything is fresh and deep.

I am dead.
I am killed:
I am being born
with the spring.

Here I have a leaf,
an ear, a whisper,
a thought:
I am going to live again,

me duelen las raíces,
el pelo,
me sonríe la boca:
me levanto
porque ha salido el sol.

Porque ha salido el sol.

the roots hurt me,
the hair,
the mouth smiles at me:
I rise
because the sun has risen.

Because the sun has risen.

XVIII
REGRESANDO

Así, pues, buenos días,
tierra sola,
soledad de este sol deshabitado
que con su nave
navega de la nieve a las espigas:
apenas despertaron
los pájaros cantores
tomó su decisión el claro día
y su campana la naturaleza.

Por eso, buenos días,
a la estabilidad, a la espesura,
del imperioso espacio
en donde tú no pasas de ser hombre
mientras te desconoce y te acaricia
la eternidad de manos transparentes.

XVIII
RETURNING

And so, good morning
lonely earth,
solitude of this abandoned sun
that with its ship
sails from snow to spikes of grain:
no sooner had
the songbirds awakened
than the clear day made its decision
and nature, its bell.

Hence, good morning
to the stability, to the thickness
of imperious space
where you are nothing more than a man
even as it does not recognize you and caresses you,
the eternity of transparent hands.

XIX
PÁJARO

Aquí en el árbol canta.

Es un pájaro solo, empedernido,
lleno de agua que cae,
de loca luz que sube,
de gutural cristal,
de trino inacabable.

Por qué?

Y la pregunta canta.

XIX
BIRD

Here in the tree it sings.

It is a solitary bird, lifelong,
full of water that falls,
of crazy light that climbs,
of guttural crystal,
of ceaseless trill.

Why?

And the question sings.

XX
El sol

Ya se sabe: la lluvia
lavó y borró los nombres.

Nadie se llama nada.

El agua impuso
en fin,
un comienzo,
una estrella apagada
en donde
no
tienen nombre
los días
ni los reinos,
ni el río.

Esto no se sabía
hasta que todos
yendo y viniendo
de sus
obligaciones
indicaban las plazas
con el dedo
y averiguaban en las librerías
la historia y geografía
de la región borrada
por la lluvia.

Hasta que el sol bajó
de su frontera

XX
The Sun

Now everyone knows: the rain
bathed and erased the names.

No one has a name.

The water imposed,
in brief,
a beginning,
an extinguished star
where the days
have
no name,
nor the kingdoms,
nor the river.

Nobody knew
until all those
going and coming
from their
obligations
were pointing at the plazas
with their finger
and were researching in the bookstores
the history and geography
of the region erased
by the rain.

Until the sun set
beyond its frontier

y fue escribiendo
nombres
amarillos
sobre todas las cosas
de este mundo.

and was writing
yellow
names
over all the things
of this world.

XXI

El llanto

Dice el hombre: en la calle he padecido
de andar sin ver, de ausencia con presencia,
de consumir sin ser, del extravío,
de los hostiles ojos pasajeros.

Dice además el hombre
que odia su *cada día* de trabajo,
su *ganarás el pan,* su triste guerra,
su ropa de oro el rico, el coronel su espada,
su pie cansado el pobre, su maleta el viajante,
su impecable corbata el camarero,
el banquero su jaula, su uniforme el gendarme,
su convento la monja, su naranja el frutero,
su carne el carnicero, el olor de farmacia
el farmacéutico, su oficio la ramera,
me dice el hombre que anda fugitivo
en el fluvial paseo del odio que ha llenado
la calle con sus pasos
rápidos, insaciables, equívocos, amargos
como si a todo el mundo la pesara en los hombros
una invisible pero dura mercadería.

Porque según me cuenta el transeúnte
se trastornó el valiente y odió la valentía,
y estuvo descontenta de sus pies la belleza
y odió el bombero el agua con que apagaba el fuego
hasta que un desgrado de algas en el océano,
un arrabal de brazos intrínsecos que llaman,

XXI
The Weeping

Man says: I have suffered in the streets
from walking without seeing, from absence with presence,
from consuming without being, from losing my way,
from hostile eyes passing by.

Man also says
he hates his *each and every day* of work,
his *you shall earn the bread,* his sad war,
the rich one his clothes of gold, the colonel his sword,
the poor one his tired foot, the traveler his suitcase,
the waiter his impeccable tie,
the banker his cage, the gendarme his uniform,
the monk his monastery, the grocer his orange,
the butcher his meat, the pharmacist
the odor of pharmacy, the whore her profession,
the man told me he walks around, a fugitive
in the riverlike passage of hate that has filled
the street with his steps
rapid, insatiable, equivocal, bitter
as though everyone bears on his shoulders the weight
of an invisible but solid commodity.

Because, according to what the passerby tells me,
the brave one became upset and hated bravery,
and the great beauty was unhappy with her feet,
and the fireman hated the water with which he was
        extinguishing the fire
such that the disgust of seaweed in the ocean,
a suburb of intrinsic arms that beckon,

---

un agitado golfo de mareas vacías
es la ciudad, y el hombre ya no sabe que llora.

a turbulent gulf of empty tides
is the city, and Man does not know it is weeping.

XXII

El que cantó cantará

Yo, el anterior, el hijo de Rosa y de José
soy. Mi nombre es Pablo por Arte de Palabra
y debo establecer mis sinrazones:
las deudas que dejé sin pagar mí mismo.

Sucede que una vez cuando ya no nacía,
cuando tal vez no fui o no fui destinado
a cuerpo alguno, incierto
entre la no existencia y los ojos que se abren,
entre cuentas de caos, en la lucha
de la material y de la luz naciente,
lo que tuve de vida fue una vacilación,
estuve vivo sin designio alguno,
estuve muerto sin nacer aún,
y entre los muros que se tambaleaban
entré a la oscuridad para vivir.

Por eso, perdón por la tristeza
de mis alegres equivocaciones,
de mis sueños sombríos,
perdón a todos por innecesario:
no alcancé a usar las manos
en las carpenterías ni en el bosque.

Viví una época radiante y sucia,
vagué sobre las olas industriales,
comiendo la ceniza de los muertos
y tanto cuando quise hablar con Dios
o con un general, para entendernos,

XXII
He Who Sang Will Sing

I, the first one, am the son of Rosa and José.
I am called Pablo, owing to the Art of the Word,
and I must lay before you my injustices:
the debts that I did not repay to myself.

It so happens that once, when I was not yet born,
when perhaps I was not or was not yet assigned
a body, uncertain
between nonbeing and eyes that open,
between stories of chaos, in the struggle
between matter and rising light,
what I had of life was a wavering,
I was alive without intention,
I was dead without yet being born,
and between walls that were shuddering
I entered the darkness to live.

That is why I ask forgiveness for the sadness
of my cheerful blunders,
of my somber dreams,
sorry, everyone, for my being useless:
I did not reach out to use my hands
in the carpentry shops or in the forest.

I lived in an epoch radiant and filthy,
I wandered over industrial waves
eating the ashes of the dead
and so often when I wanted to speak with God
or with a general, to help them understand us,

todos se habían ido con sus puertas:
no tuve adonde ir sino a mi canto.

Canto, canté, cantando
hice los números
para que ustedes sumen, los que viven
sumando,
para que resten todo
los aminoradores,
después de tanto que sobreviví
me acostumbré a morir más de una muerte.

they all had left with their doors:
I had nowhere to turn except to my song.

I sing, I sang, singing
I made up numbers
for you to add, you who live your lives
adding,
and for you bottomliners
so you might subtract everything,
after so much surviving
I have grown used to dying more than one death.

XXIII
LOS SOBERANOS

Sí, soy culpable
de lo que no hice,
de lo que no sembré, corté, medí,
de no haberme incitado a poblar tierras,
de haberme mantenido en los desiertos
y de mi voz hablando con la arena.

Otros tendrán
más luz en su prontuario,
yo había destinado a tantas cosas
crecer de mí, como de la madera
se recortan cantando los tablones,
que sin hablar de mi alma
sino mucho más tarde
yo tendré mala nota
porque no hice
un reloj: no cumplí con mi deber:
se sabe que un reloj es la hermosura.

La caracola no la puede hacer
sino la propia bestia
íntima, en su silencio,
y es propiedad de los escarabajos
la errante y enigmática estructura
de los siete relámpagos que ostentan.

Pero el hombre que sale con sus manos
como con guantes muertos
moviendo el aire hasta que se deshacen
no me merece

XXIII
The Sovereigns

Yes, I am guilty
of what I did not do,
of what I did not sow, did not cut, did not measure,
of never having rallied myself to populate lands,
of having sustained myself in the deserts
and of my voice speaking with the sand.

Others will have
more light in their criminal record,
I had destined so many things
to grow from me, as from wood
out of which the planks, singing, are cut,
and for not speaking about my soul
except much too late,
I will get a bad name
for I did not make
a clock: I have failed my duty:
it is well known, a clock is beauty.

The snail's shell can be made
only by the creature
inside it, in its silence,
and belonging only to beetles
the errant and enigmatic structure
of seven lightning bolts they show off.

But the man who leaves with his hands
as with dead gloves
moving the air until they unravel
is not worthy of

la ternura
que doy al diminuto oceanida
o al mínimo coloso coleóptero:
ellos sacaron de su propia esencia
su construcción y su soberanía.

the tenderness
I show the tiny ocean creature,
or the least colossal coleoptera:
they extracted from their own essence
their construction and their sovereignty.

XXIV
Enigma con una flor

Una victoria. Es tarde, no sabías.
Llegó como azucena a mi albedrío
el blanco talle que traspasa
la eternidad inmóvil de la tierra,
empujando una débil forma clara
hasta horadar la arcilla
con rayo blanco o espolón de leche.
Muda, compacta oscuridad de suelo
en cuyo precipicio
avanza la flor clara
hasta que el pabellón de su blancura
derrota el fondo indigno de la noche
y de la claridad en movimiento
se derraman atónitas semillas.

XXIV
Enigma with a Flower

A victory. It is too late, you did not know.
It arrived, as I willed it, like a white lily,
the white figure that penetrates
the motionless eternity of earth,
thrusting its frail but bright form
until it bores up through the clay
with a white ray of light, spur of milk.
Mute, dense darkness of the soil
in whose steep cut
the bright flower advances
until the pavilion of its whiteness
defeats the contemptible depths of the night,
and from that clarity in motion
astonished seeds scatter.

XXV
28325674549

Una mano hizo el número.
Juntó una piedrecita
con otra, un trueno
con un trueno,
un águila caída
con otra águila,
una flecha con otra
y en la pacienca del granito
una mano
hizo dos incisiones, dos heridas,
dos surcos: nació el
número.

Creció el número dos y luego
el cuatro:
fueron saliendo todos
de una mano:
el cinco, el seis,
el siete,
el ocho, nueve, el cero,
como huevos perpetuos
de un ave
dura
como la piedra,
que puso tantos números
sin gastarse, y adentro
del número otro número
y otro adentro del otro,
prolíferos, fecundos,
amargos, antagónicos,

XXV
28325674549

One hand made the number.
It joined one small stone
to another, a thunderclap
to a thunderclap,
a fallen eagle
to another eagle,
one arrow to the other
and in the patience of granite
one hand made two incisions, two wounds,
two furrows: the number
was born.

It grew, the number two and then
the four:
all were rising from
one hand:
the five, the six,
the seven,
the eight, the nine, the zero
like perpetual eggs
of a bird
hard
as stone,
which laid so many numbers
without using them up, and within
the number another number
and another within another,
wildly budding, fertile,
bitter, antagonistic,

numerando,
creciendo
en las montañas, en los intestinos,
en los jardines, en los subterráneos,
cayendo de los libros,
volando sobre Kansas y Morelia,
cubriéndonos, cegándonos, matándonos
desde las mesas, desde los bolsillos,
los números, los números,
los números.

numbering,
growing
in the mountains, in the intestines,
in the gardens, in the cellars,
falling from the books,
flying over Kansas or Morelia,
covering us, blinding us, killing us
from the tables, from the pockets,
the numbers, the numbers,
the numbers.

XXVI

LA LUNA

Yo cuento tantas cosas a mis manos
que no tienen recuerdos sino de pura seda,
de suavidad de senos o de cántaros,
que sin lucha obtuvieron,
sin cerrarse guardaron:
sin extender
semillas,
recogiendo la noche cada día,
el ovillo de aire,
hilando y deshilando la madeja
en mi delgada ineptitud:
oh manos,
dije,
levantando los brazos a la luna:
que claridad es ésta?

Tú la hiciste?

XXVI
The Moon

I tell my hands so many things
they have no memories except of pure silk,
of the smoothness of breasts or of pitchers,
which they acquired without a fight,
without tightening into a fist:
without scattering
seeds,
gathering the night each day,
the ball of air,
spinning and raveling the skein
in my fine incompetence:
O hands,
I said,
raising my arms to the moon,
what light is this?

Did you make it?

XXVII

El coro

Era en el ejercicio
del otoño extrapuro:
cuando se pudre el manto,
del oxígeno,
vacila el mundo entre el agua y la sombra,
entre el oro y el río,
y se escucha, escondida, una campana
como un pez de bronce en la altura,
hay que hablar,
hay que dar el sonido,
no importa
que se equivoque el viento:
son años de humedad,
siglos de tierra muda,
hay que contar lo que pasó en otoño,
no hay nadie:
hiere tu patrimonio sigiloso,
tu campana amarilla,
levanta tu profundidad
al coro,
que suban tus raíces
al coro:
el olvido está lleno
de gérmenes que cantan
contigo:
un gran otoño llega
a tu país
en una ola de rosas quebradas:
alguien desenterró

XXVII
The Choir

It was in the exercise
of purest autumn:
when the cloak of oxygen
rots
the world rocks between water and shadow,
between gold and the river,
it was listening to itself, a hidden bell can be heard
like a fish of bronze high up,
it must speak, it
needed to make the sound,
it is of no importance
if the wind is mistaken:
they are humid years,
centuries of mute earth,
it must be told, what happened in autumn,
there is no one:
your secret legacy wounds,
your yellow bell,
let your depths raise
the choir,
let your roots climb
to the choir,
the forgotten is riddled
with germs that sing
along with you:
in your country a grand autumn
arrives
in a wave of broken roses:
someone exhumed

todo este aroma:
es el olor del cuerpo de la tierra.

Vamos.

all of this fragrance:
it is the smell of the earth's body.

Let's go.

XXVIII
El cuerpo de la mano

Una mano es un cuerpo,
un cuerpo es una mano,
qué hacemos
con la mano del cuerpo
o el cuerpo
de la mano?
Recogimos
de tierra y mar:
sabemos
hasta el fondo,
vivimos
cuerpo a cuerpo,
y mano a mano fue la vida,
alcanzar, poseer,
tocar, entrelazar
y despedir.

XXVIII
The Body of the Hand

A hand is a body,
a body is a hand,
what do we pursue
with the hand of the body
or the body
of the hand?
We harvest
from land and sea:
we are capable
to the very bottom,
we live
body to body,
hand to hand passed life,
reaching out, possessing,
touching, weaving together
and waving goodbye.

XXIX
Nacimiento nocturno

Oh noche cenital,
directa, recta
con tu hasta ayer inaccessible
techo,
hoy eres polvareda
o beso azul,
quebranto de fulgores,
transparente tiniebla!

Amamántame,
noche,
déjame sacudir,
vaciar el líquido
de tus ubres nocturnas,
húndeme en tu regazo
horizontal, entre las poblaciones
de tu maternidad, por las moradas
de tus frías antorchas:
ir dormido en el viaje de la esfera
como un nuevo nacido, estremeciéndome
en el contacto de la desmesura
entre las lámparas de tu litoral.

XXIX
Nocturnal Birth

O highest moon,
direct, upright
with your, until yesterday, unreachable
roof,
today you are a cloud of dust
or blue kiss,
weakening of splendors,
transparent darkness!

Suckle me,
night,
let me pull,
let me empty the liquid
from your nocturnal udders,
submerge me in your horizontal
lap, among those born
of your motherhood, in the haunts
of your cold torches:
to take sleeping the sphere's journey
like a newborn, startling me
with your extravagant touch,
between the lamps of your shore.

XXX
El fondo

Poderoso del mar, desconocido
autor del movimiento,
causa en el fondo, canto,
pausada furia o cabellera rota
o ígneo motor
en agua
sepultado
como el volcán que ordena su silencio.

Es verdad que mis manos navegaron
por la extensión, ahora
confieso mi creencia:
es el abismo,
son las manos
del mar
las que me hicieron,
las que educaron
con sus guantes verdes
mis dedos
que siguen recordando
la libertad del agua.

XXX
The Bottom

Power of the sea, unknown
author of motion,
cause at the bottom, song,
slow fury or mounted defeat
or igneous engine
in water
buried
like the volcano that ordains its silence.

It's true that my hands navigated
by spreading outward, now
I confess what I believe:
the abyss exists,
the hands of the sea
are the ones
that shaped me,
those that taught
with their green gloves
my fingers
which still recall
the freedom of water.

XXXI
El viajero

Hombre para penumbra necesito,
mujer para penumbra,
en esta media tierra
estoy vencido:
yo necesito la luz más oscura:
sé que otros pueblan
la sombra indeclinable,
que la extienden
como si fuera alfombra
y de otros es la luz, el alfabeto.

Yo no descanso
en esta
latitud:
acabo de llegar:
quiero seguir el viaje.

XXXI
The Traveler

I need man for penumbra,
woman for penumbra,
on this middle earth
I am defeated:
I seek the darkest light:
I know that others populate
the shadow that cannot be refused,
that they roll it outward
as though it were carpeting
and from others comes light, the alphabet.

I will not rest
at this
latitude:
I have just arrived:
I want to resume my journey.

XXXII
La ceremonia

Qué hiciste de tus manos,
árbol muerto?
Las dejaste
colgando
del otoño?
Las arrastraste
por la carretera
de la muerte amarilla?

Oh lento nido
de la hojarasca, el viento
llegó con su violín
y luego el fuego.

Yo vi la ceremonia:
dura una vida
entera:
eres tierra, eres semilla,
eres tacto,
eres tronco,
eres hojas,
eres trino,
eres oro,
estás desnudo, encima
del invierno,
no tienes manos,
eres
de nuevo
barro,

XXXII
THE CEREMONY

With your hands, dead tree,
what did you make?
Did you abandon them
dangling
from autumn?
Did you drag them
along the road
of yellow death?

Oh slow nest
of fallen leaves, the wind
arrived with its violin
and then the fire.

I attended the ceremony:
it lasts
a whole lifetime:
you are earth, you are seed,
you are touch,
you are trunk,
you are leaves,
you are warbling,
you are gold,
you are naked, above
the winter,
you have no hands,
you are
mud
again,

silencio negro,
sombra.

black silence,
shadow.

XXXIII
Temprano

Yo soy el matinal: aquí llegó
tarde la alevosía.

Yo había hilado y deshilado el día
fresco, plateado aún de nacimiento,
y cuando Pavín Cerdo o sus parientes
letra con lepra imprimen en la charca,
qué hacerle, ya era tarde.

Sigo siendo temprano y tempranero.

XXXIII
EARLY

I am of the rites of morning: it arrived here
late, the treachery.

I was spinning and raveling the fresh
day, still silver from having been born,
and so when Pavín Cerdo or his relatives
print leprous letters on the stagnant pond,
what can be done, it is already too late.

I go on being early and rising early.

XXXIV
El uso de los días

El día es liso, suavizado,
es un ágata, es un limón,
es una uva resbalada:
su servidumbre fue partir.

De tanto salir de la noche,
de tanto volver,
se convirtió en ámbar el día,
se convirtió en materia pura.
Como en los cuchillos gastados
se afinan el mango y la hoja,
cambian de tacto,
he visto este día volver
de un largo viaje por la noche
convertido en cuchillo azul,
en herramienta de la luna.

XXXIV
Use of the Days

The day is flat, made smooth,
it is an agate, it is a lemon,
it is a slippery grape:
its duty was to depart.

From so often emerging from the night,
from so often returning,
the day turned into amber,
it turned into pure matter.
As with worn-out knives
the handle and the blade grow thin,
they change to the touch,
I have seen this day return
from a long journey through night
turned into a blue knife,
tool of the moon.

XXXV
El sello del arado

En esta tienda
quiero comprar manos,
quiero dejar
las mías:
no me sirven.

Quiero saber
si ya con tanto años
puedo
empezar otra vez,
trabajar otra vez,
continuar.
Quiero tocar con otro tacto
el mundo,
los cuerpos,
las campanas,
las raíces
nacer
en otros dedos,
crecer en otras uñas,
pero
sobre todo
cortar madera, dominar metales,
construir maestranzas, acueductos,
y triturar la tierra hasta que el polvo
y el barro nos infundan,
de tanto arar, el sello triturado
de nuestra pobre eternidad terrestre.

XXXV
Seal of the Plow

In this shop
I want to buy a pair of hands,
I want to discard
my own:
they do not serve me.

I want to know
whether being so old
I am capable
of starting over,
of working anew,
of carrying on.
With fresh feeling, I want to touch
the world,
the bodies,
the bells,
the roots,
to be born
in other fingers,
to grow in other fingernails,
but
more than anything
to cut wood, to dominate metal,
to build armories, aqueducts,
to grind up the land until the dust
and the mud infuse us—
from so much plowing, the broken seal
of our poor eternity on earth.

XXXVI
Son preguntas

Se hizo uso del cuerpo?

Era tuyo?

No era vestigio, no era un uniforme,
no fue esqueleto de la simetría,
no fue la capa impune del espíritu?

Y si copa sedienta o arma blanca
fue tu desnudo, dime
a mí, entre mis tinieblas:
la llenaste de sangre en primavera?

O buscaste otro cuerpo en que morir?

XXXVI
They Are Questions

Was use made of your body?

Was it yours?

Was it not a vestige, was it not a uniform,
was it not a skeleton of symmetry,
was it not an unpunished cape of the spirit?

And if thirsty wineglass or white weapon
were your nakedness, tell me,
in my darkness:
did you fill it with blood in springtime?

Or did you seek another body in which to die?

XXXVII
SEMEN

Porque ese grito no tiene palabra
es sólo sílaba color de sangre.

Y circula en el giro de un deseo
como un espeso manantial caliente:
sulfato de cal roja, sol secreto
que abre y cierra las olas genitales.

XXXVII
SEMEN

Because that shout has no words
it is just a syllable the color of blood.

And it circulates in the turning of desire
like a hot dense spring:
sulfate of red lime, secret sun
that opens and closes the genital waves.

XXXVIII
Es así el destino

Pero la mano busca cumplir y no en vano vuela
buscando asir: quiere tomar, tocar,
quiere ser cuerpo y morir cuerpo a cuerpo.

Estuvo en esta claridad y en la otra
buscando entre dormido y despertado
otra mano, otra rosa, otra cadera
y luego de sobrevivir al amor,
cuando se abrió y quedó sin sustancia, ya muerta,
salió a buscar la herramienta de cada día,
salió a encontrar el pan de cade calle
y tocó así las máquinas y el barro,
el cemento y la lluvia, el papel y el petróleo,
lo que corre en las aguas, lo que trae el viento,
la vida, es decir, la muerte: es decir, la vida.

XXXVIII
Such Is Destiny

But the hand seeks to fulfill and flies not in vain
seeking to grasp: it wants to take, to touch,
it wants to be body and die body by body.

It was in this clarity and in the other,
seeking between sleep and wakefulness
another hand, another rose, another hip
and then, after surviving love,
when it opened and closed with no substance, already dead,
it left to seek the tool of each day,
it left to find the bread of each street
and touched just so the machines and the mud,
the cement and the rain, the paper and the petroleum,
that which runs in the waters, that which brings the wind,
life, that is to say, death: that is to say, life.

XXXIX
Nos ahogamos

Ay que se permita padecer al feliz,
sin pegarle en el rosto con la ortiga,
sin negarle el nombre ni el vino,
sino dejarlo que toque otra tristeza:
que eche en su plato tu alma:
tenemos el deber de cargar con los otros
y hundirnos, al pasar el vado, en sangre ajena.

Es bueno que las misma aguas nos lleven,
perdiéndonos a todos, ganándonos a todos.

XXXIX
WE DROWN

Oh, may the happy man be allowed his suffering
without getting poked in the face with nettle,
without being denied his name or the wine,
without letting him touch another sadness:
may he throw your soul upon his plate:
we have a duty to bear with the others
and to fall down, to ford the river, in others' blood.

It is well that the same waters carry us,
losing us all, defeating us all.

XL
En Vietnam

Y quién hizo la guerra?

Desde anteayer está sonando.

Tengo miedo.

Suena como una piedra
contra el muro,
como un trueno con sangre,
como un monte muriendo:
es el mundo
que yo no hice.
Que tú no hiciste.
Que hicieron.
Quién lo amenaza con dedos terribles?
Quién quiere degollarlo?
Verdad que parecía estar naciendo?
Y quién lo mata ahora porque nace?

Tiene miedo el ciclista,
el arquitecto.
Se esconde la mamá con su niño y sus senos,
en el barro.
Duerme en la cueva esta mamá y de pronto
la guerra,
viene grande la guerra,
viene llena de fuego
y ya quedaron muertos,
muertos
la madre con su leche y con su hijo.

XL
In Vietnam

And who started the war?

Since the day before yesterday it resounds.

I am afraid.

It sounds like a stone
striking the wall,
like a thunderclap full of blood,
like a dying mountain:
it is the world
I did not create.
That you did not create.
That they created.
Who threatens it with terrifying fingers?
Who wants to cut its throat?
Didn't it seem it was just being born?
And who kills it now because it has been born?

The cyclist is afraid,
and the architect.
The mother hides herself, her child, and her breasts
in the mud.
She sleeps in the cave, this mother, and soon
the war,
the war comes, spreading far and wide,
it arrives full of fire
and now they are dead,
dead
the mother with her milk and her son.

Murieron en el barro.

Oh dolor, desde entonces
hasta ahora
hay que estar con el barro
hasta las sienes
cantando y disparando? Santo Dios!
Si te lo hubieron dicho
antes de ser, antes de casi ser,
si por lo menos
te hubieran susurrado
que tus parientes o tus no parientes,
hijos de aquella risa del amor,
hijos de esperma humana,
y de aquella fragancia
a nuevo lunes y a camisa fresca
tenían que morir tan repentinamente
y sin saber jamás de qué se trata!

Son los mismos
que vienen a matarnos,
sí, son los mismos
que vendrán a quemarnos,
sí, los mismos,
los gananciosos y los jactanciosos,
los sonrientes que jugaban tanto
y que ganaban tanto,
ahora
por el aire
vienen, vendrán, vinieron,
a matarnos el mundo.

They died in the mud.

What pain, from then
until now
having to remain in the mud
up to the temples
singing and shooting? God Almighty!
If they had said something to you
before this life, before you came into this life,
if only
they had whispered to you,
that your relatives or those not your relatives,
children of laughter born of love,
children of human sperm,
and of that fragrance
of a new Monday and a fresh shirt,
had to die so suddenly
without even knowing why!

They are the same ones
who come to kill us,
yes, they are the same ones
who will come to burn us,
yes, the very same ones,
the profiteers and the braggarts,
the smiling ones who were gambling so much
and who were winning so much,
now
through the air
they come, they will come, they came
to kill our world.

Han dejado una charca
de padre, madre e hijo:
busquemos
en ella,
busca tus propios huesos y tu sangre,
búscalos en el barro de Vietnam,
búscalos entre otros tantos huesos:
ahora quemados ya no son de nadie,
son de todos,
son nuestros huesos, busca
tu muerte en esa muerte,
porque están acechándote los mismos
y te destinan a ese mismo barro.

They have left behind a pool
of father, mother, and son:
we look
inside her,
she looks for your bones and your blood,
looks for them in the mud of Vietnam,
looks for them among so many other bones:
now burned they belong to no one,
they belong to everyone,
they are our bones, seek
your death in that death,
because the same ones are lying in wait for you
and they destine you to that same mud.

XLI

A PESAR

En Ecuador sale una putipintora
escribiendo mi nombre en su basura
y hoy el mundo clareaba
porque en alguna parte oscura, oscura
se divisó una estrella.

Todos llegaron a adorar la luz:
era sólo una gota de rocío.

Sin embargo la gota de rocío trabajó:
todo fue transparente:
y los oficinistas acudieron
corriendo al sitio de la claridad:
los inválidos iban a buscar
las piernas que perdieron:
las perdices dejaron en sus nidos
huevos redondeados llenos de humo
hasta que fue tan grande el aroma
y se cumplieron esperanzas
de tal manera que la tierra
se transformó en un onomástico.

Qué tristeza, en el Ecuador
una putipintora triste
rascándose su verruga
en un día tan cereal!

XLI
Despite

In Ecuador a whorish painter departs
writing my name in her rubbish
and today the world was brightening
because in some dark, dark part
a star was observed.

Everyone came to worship the light:
it was a mere drop of dew.

Nevertheless the drop of dew worked:
everything became so clear:
and the office workers came
rushing to that place of clarity:
cripples came seeking
the legs they had lost:
partridges left in their nests
round eggs full of smoke
until the aroma was so intense
and dreams were fulfilled
in such a way that the earth
became a festival of names.

Such sadness, in Ecuador
a sad whorish painter
scratching her wart
on a harvest day!

XLII

Un escarabajo

También llegué al escarabajo
y le pregunté por la vida:
por sus costumbres en otoño,
por su armadura lineal.

Lo busqué en los lagos perdidos
en el Sur negro de mi patria,
lo encontré entre la ceniza
de los volcanes rencorosos
o subiendo de las raíces
hacia su propia oscuridad.

Cómo hiciste tu traje duro?
Tus ojos de cinc, tu corbata?
Tus pantalones de metal?
Tus contradictorias tijeras?
Tu sierra de oro, tus tenazas?
Con qué resina maduró
la incandescencia de tu especie?

(Yo hubiera querido tener
un corazón de escarabajo
para perforar la espesura
y dejar mi firma escondida
en la muerte de la madera.
Y así mi nombre alguna vez
de nuevo irá tal vez naciendo
por nuevos canales nocturnos
hasta salir por fin del túnel
con otras alas venideras)

XLII

A Beetle

I also went to the beetle
and asked him about life:
about his customs in autumn,
about his linear armor.

I searched for him in the lost lakes
in the dark South of my motherland,
I found him among the ash
of the rancorous volcanoes
or climbing from the roots
toward his own darkness.

How did you make your tough suit?
Your eyes of zinc, your necktie?
Your metallic pants?
Your contradictory scissors?
Your saw of gold, your pliers?
With what resin did the radiance
of your species ripen?

(I had wanted to possess
the heart of a beetle
to pierce the thickness
and leave my signature hidden
in the death of the wood.
And so, my name will come to pass
again someday, perhaps being born
through new channels of the night
until finally leaving the tunnel
with other wings to come.)

«Nada más hermoso que tú,
mudo, insondable escarabajo,
sacerdote de las raíces,
rinoceronte del rocío»,
le dije, pero no me dijo.

Le pregunté y no contestó.

Así son los escarabajos.

"Nothing is more handsome than you
mute, inscrutable beetle,
priest of the roots,
rhinoceros of the dew,"
I said to him, but he said nothing to me.

I asked him and he did not answer.

So it goes with beetles.

XLIII
J.S.

De distraído murió Jorge Sanhueza.
Iba tan pálido en la calle
que poco a poco se perdió en sí mismo.
Y ahora cómo hallar
las lágrimas que faltan!

La verdad fue su ausencia
y aprendimos
a que se fuera retirando un poco,
un poco cada día, hasta enseñarnos
el juego de la muerte, de su muerte.

Si se escondió en el quicio de una puerta
a media luna de la noche, o bien
está detrás de una ventana oscura
haciéndonos creer que ya no existe,
yo no lo sé, tú no lo sabes, es así:
seguiremos jugando a no saberlo.

XLIII
J.S.

Of distraction Jorge Sanhueza died.
He grew so pale in the street
that little by little he became lost within himself.
And now how to find
the tears that are missing!

His absence was the truth,
and we came to understand
to what he was retiring a little,
a little each day, thus teaching us
the sport of death, of his death.

Whether he hid in the frame of a doorway
in the half moon night, or whether
he is behind a darkened window
making us believe he no longer exists,
I do not know, you do not know, so it is:
we will go on pretending not to know.

XLIV
Escribidores

El Mapús, el Mapís se preocupa,
me dicen, de mi sombra,
vive en mi sombra el pobre y se la come.
Oh gusano sombrío,
amas mi pobre sombra que yo dejo
sentada y amarrada a mi sombrero
porque olvidé, olvidamos
que este deber de tener sombra
nos viene acompañado por la luz:
y así dejé en los cines de provincia
(a la entrada) mi sombra adolescente:
luego de nave en nave la perdí,
hasta encontrarla luego
entre desnudas cestas de naranjas
o a la orilla de mar en el invierno.

Pensar que cada vez que la perdía,
mi pobre sombra aulló de abandonada
y un personaje turquestán, con cola,
vestido de plumero
y nariz puntiaguda de tijera
agusanaba su alma con mi sombra,
corroyendo su acíbar y su almíbar,
enroscándose adentro del chaleco
hasta verter mi sombra en su tintero
para escribirle a su macabro suegro
hasta pelafustarse inútilmente
y desvariar en su gusanería.

XLIV
BAD WRITERS

El Mapús, el Mapís is obsessed
they tell me, with my shadow:
the poor guy lives in my shadow and eats it.
O gloomy worm,
you love my poor shadow which I leave
seated and fastened to my hat
because I forgot, we forget
that this duty to cast a shadow
falls to us accompanied by the light:
and so I left in village cinemas
(at the entrance) my adolescent shadow:
then from ship to ship I lost it,
until I found it later
among naked baskets of oranges
or at the seashore in winter.

To think that every time I lost it,
my poor shadow howled, abandoned,
and a Turkestani, with a tail,
dressed in a feather duster,
nose pointed like scissors,
his soul worm-eaten with my shadow,
corroding his aloe and his syrup,
coiling inside his waistcoat
until pouring my shadow into his inkwell
to write to his ghoulish father-in-law
until becoming good for nothing
and delirious in his factory of worms.

XLV
Construcción a mediodía

Oh golpe en la mañana
del edificio irguiendo su esperanza:
el ruido repetido
entre el sol y los pinos
de febrero.

Alguien construye, canta
la cantera,
un cubo cae, el sol
cruza de mano en mano
en el relámpago del los martillos
y en las arenas de Punto del Este
crece una casa nueva,
torpe, sin encender y sin hablar,
hasta que el humo de los albañiles
que a mediodía comen carne asada
despliega una bandera
de rendición.

Y la casa regresa
a la paz del pinar y de la arena
como si arrepentida de nacer
se despidiera de los elementos
y quedara de pronto convertida
en un pequeño puñado de polvo.

XLV
Building at Noon

Oh pounding in the morning
from the building erecting its hope:
the sound repeated
between the sun and the pines
of February.

Someone builds, sings
the quarry,
a bucket falls, the sun
passes hand to hand
in the lightning of hammers
and on the sands of Punta del Este
a new house grows,
awkward, not lighting up and not speaking,
until the smoke of the bricklayers
who at noon eat *carne asada*
unfurls a flag
of surrender.

And the house returns
to the peace of the pines and of the sand
as though repenting having been born:
it said goodbye to the elements
and was suddenly converted
into a small handful of dust.

XLVI
El golpe

Tinta que me entretienes
gota a gota
y vas guardando el rastro
de mi razón y de mi sinrazón
como una larga cicatriz que apenas
se verá, cuando el cuerpo esté dormido
en el discurso de sus destrucciones.

Tal vez mejor hubiera
volcado en una copa
toda tu esencia, y haberla arrojado
en una sola página, manchándola
con una sola estrella verde
y que sólo esa mancha
hubiera sido todo
lo que escribí a lo largo de mi vida,
sin alfabeto ni interpretaciones:
un solo golpe oscuro
sin palabras.

XLVI
The Blow

Ink that occupies me
drop by drop
you go on guarding the trail
of my reason and my foolishness
like a great scar that will barely
be seen, when the body is sleeping
in the discourse of its destructions.

Perhaps it would have been better
had it overturned from a glass
your full essence, and sent it surging
across a single page, staining it
with a single green star
and had that stain alone
been everything
I ever wrote in my life,
with no alphabet or interpretations:
a single dark blow
without words.

XLVII

Las doce

Y me darán las mismas doce
que se dan en la fábrica,
a mí,
invitado feliz
de las arenas,
agasajado por las siete espumas
del gran océano misericorde,
a mí
me darán las mismas doce,
las mismas campanadas
que al prisionero entre sus cuatro muros,
las mismas doce horas
que al asesino junto a su cuchillo,
las mismas
doce
son para mí y para el gangrenado
que ve subir su enfermedad azul
hasta la boca quemante?

Por qué no dan mis doce del sol puro y arena
a otros mucho mejores que yo mismo?

Por qué las doce del día feliz
no se reparten invitando a todos?

Y quién dispuso para mí esta alegría
cada vez más amarga?

XLVII
The Twelve

And will they give me the same twelve
they are given at the factory,
to me,
happy guest
of the sands,
honored by the sevenfold foam
of the great compassionate ocean,
to me
will they give the same twelve,
the same strokes of a bell
they give the prisoner among his four walls,
the same twelve hours
they give the assassin with his knife,
the same
twelve
for me and for the one with gangrene
who sees his blue disease rise
to his burning mouth?

Why do they not give my twelve of pure sun and sand
to others who are much better than me?

Why are the twelve of the happy day
not widening outward to invite everyone?

And who arranged for me this joy
each time more bitter?

XLVIII
Al puente curvo de la Barra de Maldonado, en Uruguay

Entre agua y aire brilla el Puente Curvo,
entre verde y azul las curvaturas
del cemento, dos senos y dos simas,
con la unidad desnuda
de una mujer o de una fortaleza,
sostenida por letras de hormigón
que escriben en las páginas del río.

Entre la humanidad de las riberas
hoy ondula la fuerza de la línea,
la flexibilidad
de la dureza,
la obediencia impecable
del material severo.

Por eso, yo, poeta
de los puentes,
cantor de construcciones,
con orgullo
celebro
el atrio
del Maldonado, abierto
al paso pasajero,
a la unidad errante de la vida.

Lo canto,
porque no una pirámide
de osbsidiana sangrienta,
ni una vacía cúpula sin dioses,

XLVIII
The Curved Bridge of the Maldonado Bar in Uruguay

Between water and air shines the Curved Bridge:
between green and blue the curvatures
of cement, two breasts and two chasms
with the naked unity
of a woman or of a fortress,
sustained by letters of concrete
that they write on pages of the river.

Between the humanity on the banks
today the strength of the line undulates,
the flexibility
of the hardness,
the impeccable obedience
of the severe material.

For that reason, I, poet
of bridges,
singer of buildings,
with pride
celebrate
the portico
of Maldonado, open
to the fleeting footstep,
to the wandering unity of life.

I sing it,
because no pyramid
of bloodstained obsidian,
no empty cupola without gods,

ni un monumento inútil de guerreros
se acumuló sobre la luz del río,
sino este puente que hacer honor al agua
porque la ondulación de su grandeza
une dos soledades separadas
y no pretende ser sino un camino.

no useless monument to warriors
was assembled above the light of the river,
but instead this bridge that honors the water
because the rippling of its splendor
unites two separate solitudes
and does not pretend to be anything but one path.

XLIX
Casa de Mántaras en Punta del Este

Cuántas cosas caen del pino,
bigotes verdes,
música,
piñas como peñascos
o armadillos
o como libros para deshojar.

También cayó en mi cara
el pétalo sutil
que sujetaba una semilla negra:
era un ala himenóptera
del pino,
una transmigración
de suavidades
en que el vuelo se unía
a las raíces.

Caen
gotas del árbol,
puntuaciones,
vocales, consonantes,
violines,
cae lluvia,
silencio,
todo cae del pino,
del aire vertical:
cae el aroma,
la sombra acribillada
por el día,
la noche clara

XLIX
House of Mánteras in Punta del Este

So many things fall from the pine—
green mustaches,
music,
cones like craggy stones
or armadillos—
like a book about to lose its leaves.

It too fell in my face,
the subtle petal
bearing a black seed:
it was a hymenopteran wing
of the pine tree,
a transmigration
of smoothnesses
in which flight unites
with the roots.

They fall,
drops of the tree:
punctuation,
vowels, consonants,
violins,
falling rain,
silence,
everything falls from the pine,
from the vertical air:
the fragrance falls,
the shadow riddled
by the daylight,
the night clear

como leche de luna,
la noche negra
como aquella ausencia.

Amanece.

Y cae
un nuevo día
desde lo alto del pino,
cae con su reloj,
con sus agujas
y sus agujeros,
y anocheciendo cosen
las agujas del pino
otra noche a la luz,
otro día a la noche.

as milk of moon,
the night black
as that absence.

Dawn breaks.

And a new day
falls
from the top of the pine,
falls with its clock,
with its needles
and its holes,
and in the dusk
the pine needles sew
another night to the light,
another day to the night.

L
Retratos muertos

Trabajé mucho para estar inmóvil
y hasta ahora me siguen sacudiendo!
(Me susurró el difunto, y se durmió.)

Ay tanto nos movemos los humanos
que cuando el movimiento se detuvo
los demás continuaron con tu sombra
sembrándola, ay Señor, en sus batallas.

(Y los demás somos nosotros mismos
que no dejamos en paz a los muertos
lavando y refregando sus memorias,
erigiendo sin fin lo que quedó
de ellos: un patrimonio de retratos,
de bigotes y barbas que peinamos
para que estén los muertos con nosotros.)

Tanto que nos costó este movimiento
infernal, de matar hasta morir,
y ahora que nos creíamos inmóviles,
hay que salir a palos por la calle
en la resurrección de los retratos.

L
Dead Portraits

I worked hard to keep still
and even now they keep on shaking me!
(The deceased whispered to me, then fell asleep.)

Oh, we humans move so much
that when your motion ceased,
the rest, My Lord, went on sowing
your shadow among their battles.

(And the rest of us are the ones
who will not leave the dead in peace
washing and scrubbing our memories of them,
endlessly raising what remains
of them: a heritage of portraits,
of mustaches and beards we comb
so that the dead remain with us.)

This hellish movement cost us
so much, from the killing to the dying,
and now that we believed ourselves to be still
we must take to the street with sticks
in resurrection of the portraits.

LI
Esto es sencillo

Muda es la fuerza (me dicen los árboles)
y la profundidad (me dicen las raíces)
y la pureza (me dice la harina).

Ningún árbol me dijo:
«*Soy más alto que todos*».

Ninguna raíz me dijo:
«*Yo vengo de más hondo*».

Y nunca el pan ha dicho:
«*No hay nada como el pan*».

LI
It Is Simple

Strength is mute (the trees tell me)
as is profundity (the roots tell me)
as is purity (the flour tells me).

No tree ever said to me:
"I am the tallest of all."

No root ever said to me:
"I come from the very depths."

And never has the bread said:
"There is nothing like bread."

LII

Llueve en Punta del Este sobre el verde
como si se tratara de lavar,
de lavar la cabeza de los pinos.

Se enorgullece el verde con la lluvia.
Sobre el orgullo llueve de otro modo.

Llueve llorando ahora entre los pinos.

LII
The Rain

It rains in Punta del Este over the green
as though it were trying to cleanse,
to cleanse the head of the pines.

The green prides itself on the rain.
Over pride it rains in another way.

It rains, crying now among the pines.

LIII
MORALIDADES

Que la razón no me acompañe más,
dice mi compañero, y lo acompaño
porque amo, como nadie, el extravío.
Vuelve mi compañero a la razón
y acompaño otra vez al compañero
porque sin la razón no sobrevivo.

LIII
MORALS

May common sense no longer accompany me,
says my companion, and I accompany him
because I love, like no one else, going astray.
My companion regains his common sense,
and once again I accompany my companion
because lacking common sense I cannot survive.

LIV
No todo es hoy en el día

Algo de ayer quedó en el día de hoy,
fragmento de vasija o de bandera
o simplemente una noción de luz,
un alga del acuario de la noche,
una fibra que no se consumió,
pura tenacidad, aire de oro:
algo de lo que transcurrió persiste
diluido, muriendo en las saetas
del agresivo sol y sus combates.

Si ayer no continúa
en esta deslumbrante independencia
del día autoritario
que vivimos,
por qué como un portento de gaviotas
giró hacia atrás, como si titubeara
y mezclara su azul con el azul
que ya se fue?

Contesto.

Adentro de la luz
circula tu alma
aminorándose hasta que se extingue,
creciendo como un toque de campana.

Y entre morir y renacer
no hay tanto
espacio, ni es tan dura
la frontera.

LIV
Not Everything Is Now

Something of yesterday remained today,
shard of a pot or of a flag
or simply a notion of light,
algae of the aquarium of night,
a fiber that did not waste away,
pure doggedness, air of gold:
something of what has passed persists
diluted, dying by the arrows
of the aggressive sun and its battles.

If yesterday does not endure
in this dazzling independence
of the dictatorial day
in which we live,
why like a marvel of gulls
did it turn backward, as though it would stagger
and mingle its blue with the blue
that had already departed?

And I answer.

Inside the light
your soul circles
winding down until it dies out,
growing like the ringing of a bell.

And between dying and being born again
there is so little
room, nor is the frontier
so harsh.

Es redonda la luz como un anillo
y nos movemos en su movimiento.

The light is round like a ring
and we move within its movement.

LV
La sombra

Aún no vuelvo,
no he vuelto,
ando de viaje adentro
de la conflagración:
adentro de esta
vena
siguió viaje la sangre
y no puedo llegar
adentro de mí mismo.

Veo las plantas, las personas vivas,
las ramas del recuerdo,
el saludo en los ojos de las cosas,
la cola de mi perro.
Veo el silencio de mi casa, abierto
a mi voz, y no rompo las paredes
con un grito de piedra o de pistola:
ando por el terreno que conoce mis pies,
toco la enredadera que subió
por los arcos oscuros de granito
y resbalo en las cosas,
en el aire,
porque sigue mi sombra en otra parte
o soy la sombra de un porfiado ausente.

LV
The Shadow

And I still do not return,
I have not returned,
on my journey I walk
in the conflagration:
within this
vein
the blood continued its quest
and I am unable to arrive
inside myself.

I see the plants, living people,
branches of memory,
the greeting in the eyes of things,
the tail of my dog.
I see the silence of my house, open
to my voice, and I do not shatter the walls
with a shriek of stone or pistol:
I walk over terrain that knows my feet,
I touch the bindweed that climbed
through the dark granite arches
and I slip on these things,
on the air,
because my shadow persists somewhere else
or I am the shadow of the stubborn one who is missing.

LVI

UN TAL, SU PROPIA BESTIA

Fue el escritor con su pequeña bestia
sobre los hombros, siempre
creyó que eran sus alas.

Anduvo vagamente en redacciones
mostrando sus estériles
escritos, cursieróticos
versos: no
interesó, pero, cuando exhibiendo
sus credenciales, se le vio la bestia
montada sobre el hombro,
se los leyeron, y se destinó
a perpetuarse en la maledicencia.

Y le pagaron cada cuchillada.

Ya relució por fin
pero no fue firmando clara sombra,
constelación o pétalo o grandeza:
fue apresuradamente contratado
para morder, con gloria y regocijo,
y así se fue negando
a lo que fue
hasta que aquella bestia sobre el hombro,
antes inadvertida,
se convirtió en su rostro
borrando al hombre que la sostenía.

LVI
A Certain Man, His Own Beast

The writer went around with his small beast
on his shoulders, which the whole time
he believed were his wings.

He roamed aimlessly among revisions
exhibiting his sterile
works, pompous poetry
of love: he was
of no importance, but, whenever he showed
his credentials, the beast could be seen
riding on his shoulder,
they were read, and he was fated
to carry on in the slander.

And they paid him for each slash and gash.

Now, at long last, he shined
but was not inscribing a clear shadow,
constellation or petal or greatness:
he hurriedly signed on
to bite away, with glory and rejoicing,
and so he kept on denying
what he had been
until that beast on his shoulder,
having gone unnoticed,
took on his face
erasing the man who sustained it.

LVII
LAS MANOS DE LOS DÍAS

Al azar de la rosa
nace la hora iracunda
o amarilla.
Lámina de volcán, pétalo de odio,
garganta carnicera,
así es un día, y otro
es tiernamente,
sí, decididamente, epitalamio.

LVII
The Hands of the Days

By the accident of the rose
the hour is born, irascible
or yellow.
Thin layer of volcano, petal of hatred,
carnivorous throat,
such is a day, and the next one
is tenderly,
yes, resolutely, a wedding song.

LVIII
El pasado

No volverán aquellos anchos días
que sostuvieron, al pasar, la dicha.

Un rumor de fermentos
como sombrío vino en las bodegas
fue nuestra edad. Adiós,
adiós, resbalan
tantos adioses como las palomas
por el cielo, hacia el Sur, hacia el silencio.

LVIII
The Past

They will never return, those spacious days
that held up, as happiness passed by.

A rumor of ferments
like somber wine in the cellars
was our era. Goodbye,
goodbye, they slip away
so many goodbyes like doves
through the sky, toward the South, toward silence.

LIX
El vino

Ésta es mi copa, ves
brillar la sangre
detrás del filo del cristal?
Ésta es mi copa, brindo
por la unidad
del vino,
por la luz desgranada,
por mi destino y por otros destinos,
por lo que tuve y por lo que no tuve,
y por la espada de color de sangre
que canta con la copa transparente.

LIX
THE WINE

This is my glass, do you see
the blood shine
beyond the edge of the crystal?
This is my glass, I drink
to the unity
of the wine,
to the harvested light,
to my destiny and other destinies,
to what I had and what I did not have,
and to the blood-colored sword that sings
with the transparent glass.

LX
Verbo

Voy a arrugar esta palabra,
voy a torcerla,
sí,
es demasiado lisa,
es como si un gran perro o un gran río
le hubiera repasado lengua o agua
durante muchos años.

Quiero que en la palabra
se vea la aspereza,
la sal ferruginosa,
la fuerza desdentada
de la tierra,
la sangre
de los que hablaron y de los que no hablaron.

Quiero ver la sed
adentro de las sílabas:
quiero tocar el fuego
en el sonido:
quiero sentir la oscuridad
del grito. Quiero
palabras ásperas
como piedras vírgenes.

LX
VERB

I am going to crumple up this word,
I am going to twist it,
yes,
it is too flat,
it is as though a big dog or a great river
had run it over with a tongue or water
for many years.

In the word I want
roughness to be witnessed,
the salt of iron rust,
the toothless power
of the earth,
the blood
of those who spoke and those who did not speak.

I want to witness the thirst
inside the syllables:
I want to touch the fire
within the sound:
I want to feel the darkness
of the shout. I want
words rough
as virgin stones.

LXI

El canto

La mano en la palabra,
la mano en medio
de lo que llamaban Dios,
la mano en la medida,
en la cintura del alma.

Hay que alarmar las cajas del idioma,
sobresaltar hasta que vuelen
como gaviotas las vocales,
hay que amasar
el barro
hasta que cante,
ensuciarlo con lágrimas,
lavarlo con sangre,
teñirlo con violetas
hasta que salga el río,
todo el río,
de una pequeña vasija:
es el canto:
la palabra
del río.

LXI

SONG

The hand in the word,
the hand in the midst
of that which they were calling God,
the hand in the measure,
on the waist of the soul.

One must scare the boxes of language,
startling the vowels into flight
as if they were gulls,
one must knead
the mud
until it sings,
dirty it with tears,
wash it with blood,
dye it with violets
until the river flows out,
the whole river,
from a small vessel:
it is the song:
the word
of the river.

LXII
Otros dioses

Los dioses blancos duermen
en los libros:
se les ha roto el almidón, el frío
les devoró los ojos,
subsisten sin la claridad de entonces
y apenas queda una memoria
de amor entre los muslos.
La estatua quebrada
no guardó en la cintura
los relámpagos.

Se apagó la blancura.

Sin embargo, sabed, héroes cansados
de rodillas de mármol,
que el dios intransigente
de las islas marinas
o la hirsuta, emplumada
sangrienta
divinidad del África,
ceñuda en su envoltorio
o desnuda en la fiesta de la especie,
fiera tribal o corazón totémico,
tambor, escudo, lanza que vivió en la espesura
o junto a negros ríos que lloraban,
siguen ardiendo, vivos,
actuales, ancestrales,
llenos de sangre y sueños y sonidos:
aún no se sentaron en el trono
como espectros de mármol

LXII
OTHER GODS

The white gods sleep
in the books:
the starch has shattered them, the cold
devoured their eyes,
they survive without the clarity of then
and scarcely a memory remains
of love between the thighs.
The broken statue
kept no lightning bolts
around its waist.

The whiteness burned out.

Nevertheless, know ye, tired
marble-kneed heroes:
the rigid gods
of the ocean islands
or the bristly one, covered with feathers,
bloodstained
deity of Africa,
scowling in its mantle
or naked in celebration of the species,
wild tribal animal or totemic heart,
drum, shield, lance that lived in the thickness
or beside black rivers that were crying,
they went on burning, living,
modern, ancestral,
full of blood and dreams and sound:
yet they still have not sat upon the throne
like specters of marble

nacidos de la espuma,
sino que continúan en la sombra
su sombría batalla.

born of the foam,
instead they carry on in the shadows
their somber battle.

LXIII

Amigo de este invierno, y del de ayer,
o enemigo o guerrero:
frío,
a pleno sol me toca
tu contacto
de arco nevado, de irritada espina.
Con estos dedos, sin embargo,
torpes, vagos
como si se movieran en el agua,
debo desarrollar este día de invierno
y llenarlo de adioses.

Cómo agarrar en el aire el penacho
con estos dedos fríos
de muerto en su cajón,
y con los pies inmóviles
cómo puedo correr detrás del pez
que a nado cruza el cielo
o entrar en el barbecho
recién quemado, con zapatos gruesos
y con la boca abierta?

Oh intemperie del frío, con el seco
vuelo de una perdiz de matorral
y con la pobre escarcha y sus estrellas
despedazadas entre los terrones!

LXIII

WINTER

Friend of this winter, and of yesterday's,
enemy or warrior:
cold,
in full sun it touches me,
your touch
of snowy arc, of angry thorn.
And yet, with these fingers
clumsy, lazy
as though they moved in water,
I must unfurl this winter day
and fill it with goodbyes.

How to grasp the crest in the air
with icy fingers
of a dead man in his coffin,
and with these immobile feet
how can I chase the fish
that swims across the sky
or enter the fallow land
recently burned, with heavy shoes
and with my open mouth.

Oh severity of the cold, with the dry
flight of a partridge from the thicket
and with the poor frost and its stars
shattered among the clods of earth!

LXIV

El enfermo toma el sol

Qué haces tú, casi muerto, si el nuevo día lunes
hilado por el sol, fragante a beso,
se cuelga de su cielo señalado
y se dedica a molestar tu crisis?

Tú ibas saliendo de tus intestinos,
de tus suposiciones lacerantes
en cuyo extremo el túnel
sin salida, la oscuridad con su final dictamen
te esperaba: el silencio
del corazón o de otra
víscera amenazada
te hundió en la certidumbre del adiós
y cerraste los ojos, entregado
al dolor, a su viento sucesivo.

Y hoy que desamarrado de la cama
ves tanta luz que no cabe en el aire
piensas que si, que si te hubieras muerto
no sólo no hubiera pasado nada
sino que nunca cupo tanta fiesta
como en el bello día de tu entierro.

LXIV
The Patient Sunbathes

What do you do, near death, if the new Monday
spun by the sun, smelling of a kiss,
hangs itself from its outstanding sky
and devotes itself to deepening your crisis?

You were leaving your intestines,
your lacerating suppositions
in whose end the tunnel
with no exit, that darkness
with its final diagnosis,
awaits you: the silence
of the heart or of another
endangered internal organ
plunged you into the certainty of goodbyes
and you closed your eyes, surrendered
to sadness, to the wind that follows.

And on this day that cast off from the bed
you see so much light that doesn't fit in the air,
you think that if, that if you had died
nothing would have happened
barring all the rejoicing that never fit
into as beautiful a day as that of your burial.

LXV
Ya no sé nada

En el perímetro y la exactitud
de ciencias inexactas, aquí estoy, compañeros,
sin saber explicar estos vocablos
que se trasladan poco a poco al cielo
y que prueban robustas existencias.

De nada nos valió
enterrar el avestruz en la cabeza,
o hacernos agujeros en la tierra.
«No hay nada que saber, se sabe todo.»
«No nos molesten con la geometría.»

Lo cierto es que una abstracta incertidumbre
sale de cada caos que regresa
cada vez a ser orden,
y qué curioso, todo
comienza con palabras,
nuevas palabras que se sientan solas
a la mesa, sin previa invitación,
palabras detestables que tragamos
y que se meten en nuestros armarios,
en nuestras camas, en nuestros amores,
hasta que son, hasta que comienza
otra vez el comienzo por el verbo.

LXV
I Know Nothing

On the edge and in the exactitude
of inexact sciences, I am here, friends,
not knowing how to explain these vocables
that little by little make their way into the sky
and try out their vigorous lives.

We were unsuccessful
burying the ostrich in our head,
or becoming holes in the earth:
"There is nothing more to know, everything is known."
"Trouble us no longer with geometry."

It is certain that an abstract uncertainty
takes leave of each chaos that returns
each time to order,
and how curious, everything
begins with words,
new words that sit alone
at the table, not having been invited,
hateful words that we swallow
and that get into our cupboards,
our beds, our loves,
until they exist: until the beginning
begins again in the verb.

LXVI
ARRABALES

Andando por San Antonio arriba
vi la quietud de la pobreza:
rechinaban los goznes quebrados,
las puertas cansadas querían
ir a sollozar o a dormir.
Debajo de los cristales rotos
en las ventanas, alguna flor,
un geranio amargo y sediento,
sacaba a pasear por la calle
su anaranjado fuego sucio.

Los niños del silencio aquel
desde sus ojos negros me vieron
como mirando desde un pozo,
desde las aguas olvidadas.

De pronto entró por la calle el viento
como si buscara su casa.

Se movieron los papeles muertos,
el polvo, perezosamente,
cambió de sitio, se agitó
un trapo en la ventana rota
y todo siguió como estaba:
la calle inmóvil, los ojos
que me miraron desde el pozo,
las casas que no parecían
esperar a nadie, las puertas
ya demolidas y desnudas:
todo era duro y polvoriento:

LXVI

SUBURBS

Walking high up, through San Antonio
I witnessed the quietude of poverty:
the broken hinges were creaking,
the tired doors were wanting
to go off to sob or to sleep.
Beneath the cracked crystals
in the windows, some flower,
a bitter and thirsty geranium,
took for a walk in the street
its dirty orange fire.

The children of that silence
from their black eyes watched me
as though looking from a well,
from the forgotten waters.

Suddenly the wind entered the street
as though searching for its house.

The dead papers stirred,
the dust, lazily,
rearranged itself, a rag
flapped in the broken window,
and everything carried on as it was:
the motionless street, the eyes
that watched me from the well,
the houses that never seemed
to wait for anyone, the doors
already demolished and naked:
everything was hard and dusty:

estaba muerto, estaba vivo,
quería morir y nacer.

Se preparaba para el fuego
la madera de la pobreza.

it was dead, it was alive,
it wanted to die and be born.

It readied itself for the fire,
the wood of poverty.

LXVII
El regalo

De cuántas duras manos
desciende la herramienta,
la copa,
y hasta la curva insigne
de la cadera que persigue luego
a toda la mujer con su dibujo!

Es la mano que forma
la copa de la forma,
conduce el embarazo del tonel
y la línea lunar de la campana.

Pido unas manos grandes
que me ayuden
a cambiar el perfil de los planetas:
estrellas triangulares
necesita el viajero:
constelaciones como dados fríos
de claridad cuadrada:
unas manos que extraigan
ríos secretos para Antofagasta
hasta que el agua rectifique
su avaricia perdida en el desierto.

Quiero todas las manos de los hombres
para amasar montañas
de pan y recoger
del mar todos los peces,
todas las aceitunas
del olivo,

LXVII
The Gift

From so many rough hands
descended the tool,
the wineglass,
even the famous curve
of the hip that then pursued
the whole woman with its design!

The hand that forms
the wineglass of the form,
it conveys the pregnancy of the barrel
and the lunar line of the bell.

I ask some mighty hands
to help me
change the profile of the planets:
triangular stars
the traveler needs:
constellations like cold dice
of square clarity:
those hands that extract
secret rivers for Antofagasta
until the water rectifies
its avarice lost in the desert.

I want all the hands of men
to knead mountains
of bread and to gather
all the fish from the sea,
all the olives
from the olive tree,

todo el amor que no despierta aún
y dejar un regalo
en cada una de las manos
del día.

all the love not yet wakened
and to leave a gift
in each of the hands
of the day.

LXVIII
La bandera

Dale un golpe de fuego a tu guitarra,

levántala quemando:

es tu bandera.

LXVIII
THE FLAG

Strike a blow of fire with your guitar,

raise it, as it burns:

it is your flag.

Pablo Neruda was born Neftalí Ricardo Reyes Basoalto in Parral, Chile, in 1904. He served as consul in Burma and held diplomatic posts in various East Asian and European countries. In 1945, a few years after he joined the Communist Party, Neruda was elected to the Chilean Senate. Shortly thereafter, when Chile's political climate took a sudden turn to the right, Neruda fled to Mexico and lived as an exile for several years. He later established a permanent home at Isla Negra. In 1970 he was appointed Chile's ambassador to France, and in 1971 he was awarded the Nobel Prize in Literature. Pablo Neruda died in 1973.

About the Translator

William O'Daly has previously published six books of the late and posthumous poetry of Pablo Neruda with Copper Canyon Press, as well as a chapbook of his own poems, *The Whale in the Web*. His eighth Neruda translation, *World's End* (*Fin de Mundo*, 1969) is forthcoming from Copper Canyon Press in late 2008. O'Daly was a finalist for the 2006 Quill Award in Poetry for *Still Another Day*, the first book of his Neruda series. A National Endowment for the Arts Fellow, he has worked as a literary and technical editor, a college professor, and an instructional designer, and his poems, translations, essays, and reviews have appeared in a wide range of magazines and anthologies. With co-author Han-ping Chin, he recently completed a historical novel, *This Earthly Life,* set during the Chinese Cultural Revolution. O'Daly lives with his wife and daughter in the Sierra Nevada foothills of California.

OTHER BOOKS BY PABLO NERUDA
FROM COPPER CANYON PRESS

Still Another Day
The Separate Rose
Winter Garden
Stones of the Sky
The Sea and the Bells
The Yellow Heart
The Book of Questions

The Chinese character for poetry is made up of two parts: "word" and "temple." It also serves as pressmark for Copper Canyon Press.

Since 1972, Copper Canyon Press has fostered the work of emerging, established, and world-renowned poets for an expanding audience. The Press thrives with the generous patronage of readers, writers, booksellers, librarians, teachers, students, and funders—everyone who shares the belief that poetry is vital to language and living.

Major funding has been provided by:
Anonymous (2)
Sarah and Tim Cavanaugh
Beroz Ferrell & The Point, LLC
Lannan Foundation
National Endowment for the Arts
Cynthia Lovelace Sears and Frank Buxton
Washington State Arts Commission

For information and catalogs:
COPPER CANYON PRESS
Post Office Box 271
Port Townsend, Washington 98368
360-385-4925

www.coppercanyonpress.org

This book was designed and typeset by Phil Kovacevich.
The typeface is Sabon, designed by Jan Tschichold in 1964.

9 781556 592720